150 NOT OUT

The story of the PAYMASTER GENERAL'S OFFICE 1836 - 1986

COLIN ULPH

Original photographs by Ken Bridle

HER MAJESTY'S PAYMASTER GENERAL'S OFFICE, CRAWLEY

British Library Cataloguing in Publication Data

Great Britain *Paymaster General*

150 not out: the story of the Paymaster General's Office, 1836-1986
1. Great Britain, *Paymaster General* — History
I. Title *II. Ulph, Colin*
345.410072 *HJ1036*

ISBN 0 9510433 0 7

HM PAYMASTER GENERAL'S OFFICE,
SUTHERLAND HOUSE, RUSSELL WAY,
CRAWLEY, WEST SUSSEX RH10 1UH

Typeset by Blackmore Typesetting, Hove
Printed by New England Press Ltd, Hove
Bound by Kensett Ltd, Hove

Cover photo of Sutherland House, by Ken Bridle, 1985

CONTENTS

PAYMASTER GENERAL JOHN GUMMER is shown computer equipment by shift leader Barry Bartholomew, during a visit in December 1984. Looking on are Alf McClatchey (Head of Computer and Banking Services), Alex Galloway (private secretary to Mr Gummer), Laurie Andrews (Assistant Paymaster General) and Dennis Breed (Head of Pensions and Administration).

Photo: Ken Bridle.

FOREWORD :

by John Selwyn Gummer MP, Paymaster General

Britain has always managed to make the new more homely and to accustom us to technological change by clothing it in the trappings of the past. So, where others would establish a payments arm of the Treasury, we have happily retained the Paymaster General's Office and still made it measurably one of the most efficient Departments in Government. From high stools and hand-drawn drafts in Whitehall to fully computerised pension payment in Crawley — the Paymaster General's Office has come a long way in 150 years. The Bill which was to cause its demise in the Nineteenth Century was passed yet never enacted and the efficiency studies of our own times found that it did its job too cost-effectively to lose its independent existence.

No wonder we're proud of this odd corner of Government which is central to so many people's lives. Pensioners and payroll; farmers and military men have reason to rely on our regularity and we pride ourselves too on our ability to deal with the unusual — the special arrangement and the awkward case. In amongst all those computers there are people who take pleasure in providing a personal service and in continuing 150 years of tradition.

John Selwyn Gummer

House of Commons
June 1985

PREFACE

One of the least known of all government departments, the Paymaster General's Office has been quietly going about the essential business of paying the nation's bills for almost a century and a half, seeking neither publicity nor plaudits. Apart from our official contacts and the folk who receive pensions from us, there must be very few citizens who know that we even exist, and still fewer who appreciate our functions and long history. Sutherland House, like our many earlier offices, delights in anonymity: its fortress-like appearance seems almost to defy recognition as the current home of a department with vital functions, and roots in the age of Oliver Cromwell.

Yet the PGO has no reason to be modest. Over the years it has established in government circles a reputation for reliability, accuracy and efficiency which is second to none, while the service offered to pensioners is such as to be taken for granted. Today the justification for a single office making all government payments is even sounder than it was when the original pay offices merged in 1836: in this age of technology the PGO is able to issue pensions to over a million public servants, process 30 million transactions a year and handle over £250 billion annually, while remaining one of the smallest departments. It is therefore high time that our history and achievements were put on record, and fitting that our 150th anniversary should provide the opportunity.

Compiling this book has proved a fascinating and rewarding experience. Inevitably it has unearthed a succession of dates and statistics, but also it has brought me into contact with scores of people with vivid memorites of the personalities, events and working conditions of the past. What emerges, I hope, is a picture of the life and times of not just an office but a tiny community, where experiences in good times and bad are shared with colleagues and friends.

I am grateful to all who have helped to supply material, especially those who spared the time for a lengthy chat reliving the old days. My thanks and appreciation go also to the former Paymasters General who spoke to me about their terms of office; Lord Congleton for sharing his knowledge of Sir Henry Parnell; the staff of the Public Record Office, House of Lords Record Office, Museum of London, Imperial War Museum, National Portrait Gallery, Department of the Environment Property Services Agency, International Computers Ltd, Crawley News and the Guildhall, Holborn and Crawley libraries for their assistance and/or permission to reproduce photographs; Ken Bridle for enhancing the book with his excellent original photography; Jane Wiscombe for typing the draft; all who have read it over and suggested corrections; and finally my family and my staff in TP division who have had to cope with my frequent absences and silences while engaged on the project.

I am well aware that more remains to be told. In a volume of this size I have been able to merely scratch the surface of events which, with further research, could warrant a book of their own. Maybe my efforts will whet the appetite of some future historian and inspire a more thorough study of particular periods. For the present, I hope that this book will help current staff to appreciate their heritage, revive memories for retired colleagues and give the citizens of Crawley an insight of what goes on within the anonymous grey fortress they still call 'Alcatraz'.

Sutherland House
June 1985

1. ROOTS : *the road to 1836*

Four beginnings

Although it was in 1836 that the Paymaster General's Office came into being as a new government department with its own political head, there was nothing new about its functions. To use the term in the enabling Act of 1835 the creation of the PGO was a 'consolidation', bringing together four pay offices which had been in existence already for at least 150 years within various branches of the armed services. In that time all four offices had acquired distinctive duties, practices and traditions which were to be carried forward into the new, consolidated office. The roots of the PGO are entwined therefore in both naval and military history in a particularly active age, and in the evolving British system of banking, accounting and pensions. In this chapter we shall identify some of the milestones along the road to 1836, and the influence exerted by some of the better known and more colourful characters of the period.

Even before the Civil War of 1642-51 there were army officers called 'paymasters' whose duty was to defray the expenses of specific military campaigns. There being then no permanent British army there was no post or office with overall responsibility for the paymasters. However, in 1649 Cromwell created two posts of Treasurer at War to pay the expenses of his newly-formed parliamentary army, and although these disappeared when that army was disbanded at the Restoration they were replaced in 1660 by the overall paymaster in the first standing army of Charles II. Initially the post was entitled Receiver and Paymaster of the Guards, but soon it became Paymaster General of the Guards and Garrisons, then Paymaster General of the Guards, Garrisons and Land Forces and by 1743, simply **PAYMASTER GENERAL OF THE FORCES.** This officer, always a leading member of the government of the day, employed a small staff of clerks and other personnel to carry out the day-to-day administration on his behalf. They were the predecessors of the PGO.

In 1682 Charles founded the Chelsea Hospital 'for the relief of such Land Soldiers as are or shall be old, lame or infirme in ye service of the Crowne', an enterprising venture by the Merry Monarch which aimed to promote recruitment by promising some light at the end of the tunnel of a soldier's army career. Unfortunately no support was forthcoming from parliament, so it was to secure much-needed finance for the project as well as to establish a link between the hospital and the army that Charles appointed a wealthy ex-Paymaster General of the Forces to be the first **PAYMASTER AND TREASURER OF CHELSEA HOSPITAL.** Soon it became the normal practice for the same individual to hold both this and the post of Paymaster General of the Forces.

For about 200 years after the Civil War, the Board of Ordnance, responsible for military stores, weapons, ammunition and the pay of the artillery and engineers, was quite separate from either the army or the navy. The **TREASURER OF THE ORDNANCE** was first appointed in 1670, to make payments to contractors, civilian staff and ordnance troops. His was the third of the four offices to be absorbed by the consolidation.

The fourth was the oldest. The title **TREASURER OF THE NAVY** had existed since the reign of Henry VIII, and until the 17th century such importance was attached to it that the post was invariably held by the most senior member of the Navy Board. Later it became more independent of the main stream of navy politics, and by 1836 the navy pay office was ripe for amalgamation with those of the army, ordnance and Chelsea Hospital.

Patronage and profits

A study of the politics and conduct of the nation's finances in the 17th century reveals a sorry tale of patronage, inefficiency, incompetence and sometimes downright dishonesty. Although a parliament existed, it was not strong enough to prevent the Stuart kings from running up huge debts, spending their revenues without keeping proper account, handing out top jobs in settlement of debts or repayment for services rendered, and making appointments to 'sinecure' offices which earned their holder a tidy income without his actually having to do anything. All revenues belonged to the Crown, and it was the Crown which made appointments of officials such as the Paymaster General of the Forces and the Treasurers of the Navy and the Ordnance. The importance of these offices cannot be over-emphasised, for this was an age when the armed services were engaged almost continuously in war with one or other of the king's enemies; consequently vast sums of money were passing through the hands of the Paymasters and Treasurers. Yet often, in selecting individuals to fill these sought-after posts, scant regard was paid to either administrative ability or integrity of character. Many were the Paymasters who fell short of the standards which the sovereign, the public, and the services might have expected.

The first Treasurer of the Navy and the first Paymaster General after the Restoration were both selected by Charles II out of gratitude for special service during the Civil War; both had to be found seats in parliament hastily in order to get them into British politics at such a senior level; and while in office both accumulated a sizeable fortune. Charles's choice as Treasurer of the Navy was Sir George Carteret. A most loyal supporter and close friend, Carteret was undoubtedly a fine sailor and a brave man. During the Civil War he had executed daring naval exploits around the coast of his native Jersey, had twice given sanctuary on that island to Charles when all seemed lost on the mainland, and had carried on a resistance movement from France when finally forced to surrender Jersey to the parliamentary forces. Already kingly rewards had been showered upon him in the shape of the Lieutenant-governorship of Jersey and the grant of lands in the New World to be named 'New Jersey', but in 1660 Carteret's determination brought him the prize he sought above all others: he became Treasurer of the king's navy. Unfortunately for Carteret, and for the navy, he was no book-keeper. During the time of the Great Plague he had to borrow money on his own credit in order to keep the navy afloat, and in 1667 the Commissioners for the Public Accounts had to report on 'gross mismanagement' in the navy and particularly 'carelessness in keeping the accounts'. Carteret managed to secure an exchange of posts with the Earl of Anglesey and became Deputy Treasurer of Ireland, but he could not evade the consequences of his shortcomings. In 1669 he was suspended from the House of Commons by 100

SIR STEPHEN FOX, Paymaster General of the Forces 1660-79, from a portrait by P Lely.
Reproduced by permission of the National Portrait Gallery.

votes to 97 (clearly he had some supporters left), and escaped further action only by the prorogation of parliament.

For his Paymaster General of the Forces, the king chose Stephen Fox, a man who had helped to organise Charles's escape from Shoreham after the Battle of Worcester in 1651, and had managed the royal household during the period of exile. In 1658 he was the one to bring Charles the glad tidings of Cromwell's death. Fox was rather better equipped for his new post than was Carteret, for at least he had been trained in book-keeping. Sir Stephen Fox (he was knighted in 1665) was to serve as Paymaster General for 19 years — longer than any other to the present day. By the time he surrendered the post he was estimated to be worth more than £200,000. Some of this fortune was later put to good use when Charles appointed him to be Treasurer of the newly-founded Chelsea Hospital: Fox is reputed to have donated £13,000 towards its building and maintenance. Without such support, and that of Sir Christopher Wren, who received nothing for his design of the buildings, the king's Hospital scheme would have surely foundered, for Charles received not a penny from parliament.

One of the reasons that the posts of Paymaster General of the Forces and Treasurer of the Navy proved so lucrative to their fortunate holders was that until 1782 it was the accepted practice that whatever funds these gentlemen deemed to need for the expenses of the armed services were paid over to them personally. There was no check on how they used the money, or even whether they spent it at all, and even the most honest of Paymasters quite openly made use of the balance while it remained in his hands. Thus considerable interest was earned by these gentlemen until (or unless) the funds came to be spent on the services for which they had been released by the Exchequer. In 1667 an Act of parliament set out to charge interest on moneys held for the Crown by certain officials but which were being used 'for their private lucre and advantage'. However there was no specific mention of the Paymaster General or the Treasurer of the Navy, who handled the largest amounts of all, and of course no indication that there might have been anything unethical in what they were doing.

Not until 1831 did parliament call for an account of how money voted to the Admiralty was spent, and it was 1846 before equivalent 'appropriation accounts' were demanded for the army and ordnance services. Therefore there was every incentive in the 17th century for Paymasters to retain public money in their own pockets: indeed, it was the acknowledged custom until 1780 that an outgoing Paymaster took with him any unspent funds, a fresh amount being granted to his successor. Parliament under Charles II did appoint commissioners 'to take and state the Public Accounts', and these reported at irregular intervals for nearly 50 years. But however well intentioned, the commissioners proved to be less independent and effective than they should have been, and showed merely what had been obvious all along: that officials like the Paymaster General were insufficiently accountable to anyone but themselves. Nevertheless, as we have seen, they did severely embarrass Sir George Carteret in 1667, and 35 years later one of their reports was to cause the downfall of the Irish peer, the Earl of Ranelagh, who was Paymaster General 1689 - 1703.

Having in 1670 inveigled Charles II into allowing him to administer the finances of Ireland, and having so impoverished that province by arbitrary taxation and misapplication of revenues that the Lord Lieutenant refused to pass his accounts, Ranelagh had a writ filed against him by the attorney general, with the result that the king ordered that he should receive no further payments. Against this sort of background it seems incredible that only 10 years later Ranelagh was appointed privy councillor and Paymaster General. Not surprisingly he carried incompetence and lack of integrity into his new office, but even so managed to hold on to the job for 12 years.While Treasurer of Chelsea Hospital he built himself a handsome house within the grounds and acquired the freehold of some 22 acres of land at a ground rent of £5, wherein he laid out landscaped gardens which were to become a fashionable resort after his death. By 1702 the Public Accounts Commissioners were on to him , and Ranelagh resigned in an effort to forestall further action. However, the enquiries were pursued, the examination of his accounts taking over three years. The auditors had particular difficulty with the account for 1701, and disallowed upwards of £4½ million for want of proper vouchers. In 1703 Ranelagh was expelled from parliament after a conviction for misappropriating £72,000. Even then he was not finished, for the following year Queen Anne was graciously pleased to appoint him as one of the governors of her Bounty for the augmentation of the maintenance of poor clergymen. It is some consolation, however, to know that Ranelagh died in 1711 a destitute man, still pursued by his debtors.

In 1689, after a bloodless revolution, came the installation of William and Mary as joint sovereigns with powers greatly curtailed by an emergent parliament. During their reign came a flood of measures which were to transform the face of British finance. The National Debt came into being to raise funds to fight the French, the Bank of England was established and Exchequer bills were introduced. The supply of funds for the army, navy and ordnance became an annual rather than an *ad hoc* affair, and parliament determined to vote a fixed sum to the monarch which included allowance for expenditure on civil government: this was the origin of the 'civil list'.

In 1700-3 were passed three further Acts designed to get the Paymasters General and Treasurers to account for interest earned by them on imprested money, and to submit their accounts for audit. The 1702 measure proclaimed in no uncertain fashion that it was 'An Act for making good Deficiencies, and for preserving the publick Credit'; the 1703 Act set out to obviate the 'mischief' caused by officials, like Ranelagh, who left their accounts so incomplete that the auditors found it impossible to calculate the interest due. In the light of all this it was strange that after 1713 there was no reappointment of the Commissions for Public Accounts, until 1779. Possibly the explanation was that a long and unaccustomed period of peace was in progress and the nation was spending less money. Audit was left in the rather ineffectual hands of an official called the Auditor of the Imprest, who apparently unearthed nothing of any note.

During the 18th century the quality of Paymasters and Treasurers varied widely. Four of them, Robert Walpole, Spencer Compton, Henry Pelham and Lord North went on to become First Lord of the Treasury (later known as Prime Minister), while William Pitt (the Elder) had a nine year spell as Paymaster General before emerging as the nation's leader in all but title. It was the honest Pitt who caused a mild sensation by refusing to use for his own profit the vast sums of money which passed through his hands as Paymaster General, or to accept the commission which foreign rulers had traditionally paid his predecessors in return for subsidies. While Treasurer of Chelsea Hospital Pitt brought in a Bill for the relief of the Hospital's 'maimed and worn out Soldiers' which passed through both Houses without opposition and received the royal assent within a month. At least two gentlemen combined their office with that of Speaker of the Commons. Spencer Compton was Paymaster General for five years of his 12 year spell as Speaker, while Arthur Onslow's term of 33 years as Speaker included eight when he was also Treasurer of the Navy.

A much less honourable man was Stephen Fox's youngest son, Henry (later Lord Holland). Here was a man certainly in the right place at the right time, for his term as Paymaster General (1757-65) largely coincided with the dates of the Seven Years War, when record sums were being voted for army expenses. Being a man of little principle or regard for the opinion of others, Holland seized with open arms this heaven-sent opportunity to amass a personal fortune, and by the time he left office he had accrued £250,000 of public money. Holland was dead by the time his sins found him out, and when the reconstituted Public Accounts Commission reported in 1780 it was his unfortunate executors who had to make repayment to the Exchequer.

The idea of reactivating the Accounts Commissions was quite probably generated by the deeds of Richard Rigby, last of the really dishonourable

HENRY FOX (LORD HOLLAND), Paymaster General of the Forces 1757-65; artist after Sir Joshua Reynolds.
Reproduced by permission of the National Portrait Gallery.

Paymasters General. Rigby became an MP on the back of a wealthy patron, wormed his way into the paymastership, 'the avowed goal of his ambition' according to a friend, and proceeded to accumulate around £½ million of public money. When the attorney general demanded repayment of the misappropriated funds Rigby expressed amazement, and contrived to avoid impeachment by acts of the grossest bribery. While Paymaster General he regularly threw lavish and rowdy parties at the office which were attended by senior Ministers of the government and no doubt helped to secure his 14 year tenure of the post. According to one contemporary he had a very expressive countenance in which 'all the comforts of the pay office' were depicted, and such was the reputation he left behind that many years later Benjamin Disraeli would use the term 'Rigby' to describe corrupt and parasitic politicians to whom he took a dislike. In view of the damage that this shameless man did to the good name of the office it was just as well that he was the last of his kind, the last to make huge profits out of his position. One wonders whom W S Gilbert had in mind when he gave to Pooh Bah (Lord High Everything Else) the immortal line in 'The Mikado':-

> *As Paymaster General I could so cook the accounts that, as Lord High Auditor, I should never discover the fraud.*

Burke's laws

By now the country was more than ready to respond to a movement for economical reform pioneered by the energetic and eloquent Irishman, Edmund Burke. Burke had come to England at the age of 21 to study law, but instead of being called to the bar he obtained employment as private secretary to eminent politicians and eventually became a member of parliament. Although because of his inferior background he was never quite accepted as an equal by his Whig colleagues, nevertheless Burke was a man of vision and a master of the written and spoken word whose opinions were forthright, honestly held and ignored at one's peril. He championed the cause of the revolting American colonies, supported the abolition of the slave trade and was the first to warn of the dangers of the French Revolution. In 1778 he turned his attention to the reform of government finance.

Having pumped good money after bad into the ill-fated American campaign, Britain desperately needed to take every advantage of the new wealth being offered by the Industrial Revolution. Yet Burke saw public money being squandered on sinecure offices created by the king (George III) to reward his creditors or friends; he saw revenues being spent without proper accounting or audit; and he saw senior officials like the Paymaster General growing fat on moneys which should have been retained in the public purse. In one famous incident in the House in 1778 his fiery temper gave way to deeds rather than words. In a debate on the navy estimates when Lord Mulgrave of the Admiralty admitted that 'not a shilling' had been spent on the purpose for which it had been voted, Burke seized hold of the estimates book and hurled it in the direction of the Treasury bench, narrowly missing the shins of Welbore Ellis, the Navy Treasurer.

Edmund Burke was still an opposition MP when in 1780 he introduced no less than five Bills aimed at 'retrenchment' and economical reform. One of these aimed to divert into the coffers of the nation the profits made by Paymasters General. Although received with predictably lukewarm enthusiasm by the government of Lord North, Burke's fervour did succeed in reviving the Accounts Commissions. Reconstituted, with enlarged terms of reference, the commissioners set to work with a will, producing 14 reports in the next seven years. Ominously for ex-Paymasters General and Treasurers of the Navy, the commissioners were instructed to report 'what Balances are in the Hands of Accountants which may be applied to the public Service'. In their 3rd and 4th reports they duly uncovered the sum of £454,582.3s.8¼d. lying in the hands of former Paymasters General or Navy Treasurers (or their executors, six of them having since died), and in 1781 an Act was passed which actually named the offenders. These included the deceased Lord Holland, leading the way with over £256,000 and the current Prime Minister Lord North who had been rash enough to set up the commission in the previous year.

The commissioners had reported that the main cause of the large balances was the practice of keeping a cash balance for each 'head' of service, rather than treating all sums received for the army or navy as belonging to one account and using unspent balances under one head to make payments from another. This was a significant finding by the Accounts Commission for the reduction of cash balances was to be the prime justification for the consolidated Paymaster General's Office 55 years later. The report went on to recommend that this 'Public Money, long ago issued, and still remaining in their Hands may, with all

ANNO VICESIMO SECUNDO

Georgii III. Regis.

* *

C A P. LXXXI.

An Act for the better Regulation of the Office of Paymaster General of His Majesty's Forces.

WHEREAS it appears, by the Reports made by the Commissioners appointed to examine, take, and state the publick Accounts of the Kingdom, that the Paymasters of the Forces have heretofore been accustomed to accumulate large Sums of Publick Money in their Hands, beyond what was necessary for carrying on the Services in their Department, and to take and carry out of Office with them, upon their Resignation or Removal, large Balances of Publick Money, which they have retained and kept in their Hands many Years after being out of Office: And whereas it is highly expedient that a Remedy should be provided for these Inconveniencies; be it therefore enacted by the King's most Excellent Majesty, by and with the Advice and Consent of the Lords Spiritual and Temporal, and Commons, in this present Parliament assembled, and by the Authority of the same, That from and

Preamble.

13 X 2 after

8

PREAMBLE TO THE PAYMASTER GENERAL ACT 1782.

convenient Speed, be restored to the Possession of the Public'. So the 1781 Act directed that these sums should be repaid to the Exchequer within six months, and the luckless Paymasters or their executors had no alternative but to comply.

Burke's other measures were lost on a narrow vote, but by 1782 the Whigs had gained power on the resignation of North. Possibly he had hoped for higher things, but to Edmund Burke, ironically, fell the non-Cabinet office of Paymaster General of the Forces. To his everlasting credit, Burke decided to continue his purge of the pay office. He began, like Pitt the Elder, by refusing to accept into his own account the substantial funds allocated to the army. Instead, he took an annual salary of £4,000 a year and paid the army's balances into the Bank of England, so that the nation and not the Paymaster General gained the benefit of interest earned. Previous Treasurers of Chelsea Hospital had taken for themselves the profits arising from the supply of clothes to the pensioners: Burke directed these also into the public purse and managed to save still more by making a fresh agreement with the suppliers.

Then he set about drafting a Bill 'for the better Regulation of the Office of Paymaster General of his Majesty's Forces'. Burke himself presented this to the Commons on 26 June 1782, and having passed through all the usual stages in both Houses, it received the Royal Assent only 15 days later, on 11 July. The Act began by reciting the customary but now unacceptable practices of the earlier Paymasters, and went on to specify measures to ensure that public money remained the property of the public and was not used to line the pockets of politicians. Henceforward all moneys issued for army services would be paid into the Bank of England; when a Paymaster General required any of it he was to state how much and for what purpose it was required; statements of balances were to be prepared monthly; and outgoing Paymasters were to hand over the balances to their successors.

There were other provisions of interest, including the creation of a fund financed by fees received at the pay office, in order to provide for annual pay rises for employees and increases in the half pay and widows and childrens pensions payable by Chelsea Hospital. The Act also made it clear that any person forging the signature of the Paymaster General or his deputy 'shall suffer Death as in Cases of Felony, without benefit of Clergy'. This punishment was reduced to 14 years transportation in an Act of 1807. Some of the Act's provisions having been found 'inconvenient' by the following year, most of its general principles were re-enacted in 1783, with alterations to detailed procedures. Among the new provisions were that the pay office staff should receive annual salaries, payable quarterly.

While in government Burke did not neglect the other measures he had advanced when in opposition. He steered through a measure popularly called 'Burke's Act' which gave the Treasury control over payments from the civil list and abolished a dozen government offices in the name of economy, efficiency and security. Several sinecure offices were among the victims, including the quaintly named offices of the Great Wardrobe, the Master of the Stag Hounds and the Board of Green Cloth. More surprisingly, the Act abolished also the Board of Trade, Board of Works, Secretary of State for the Colonies and the 'Paymaster of the Pensions'. In a later chapter we shall trace the history and development of public service pensions: suffice to say here that at this time the Paymaster General paid no pensions except those of the Chelsea Hospital and of course retired and half pay to army officers.

EDMUND BURKE, Paymaster General of the Forces 1782 and 1783; studio of Reynolds.
Reproduced by permission of the National Portrait Gallery.

It seems incredible that Edmund Burke was in office for only four months, resigning in July 1782 rather than serve under a new Prime Minister. Although he was back the following year, his second tenure lasted only nine months. Yet in these two brief spells he ably demonstrated the standards which parliament and the public have since come to expect from persons in high office, and he pointed the way to new concepts in the handling and control of public money.

At the time of Burke we find one of the earliest mentions by name of permanent officials at the army pay office. John Powell and Charles Bembridge were respectively Cashier and Accountant, the two senior officers after the Paymaster General and his deputy. In 1780 they had given invaluable assistance to the Accounts Commission in establishing the size of the balances held by earlier Paymasters, and in 1782 they aided Edmund Burke in implementing reforms within the office. Burke's successor, Isaac Barre, showed singular ingratitude by having them both suspended, on charges of corruption. Burke believed that there were political motives in their removal, and on regaining office in April 1783 he reinstated them, even though charges were still pending. This generated a heated debate in the Commons, during which Burke had to be pulled down by the coattails to stop his invective against the critics. Unfortunately, there is no record of what became of Powell and Bembridge after the controversy.

After Burke

After Burke's departure the process of financial reform continued. In 1785 a new Act laid down regulations for the office of the Treasurer of the Navy, similar to those in force for the Paymaster General of the Forces. The following year saw the creation of the Consolidated Fund, which allowed all revenues to be credited to a single fund, and for all payments to be made from only one account. This measure was to greatly simplify government accounting, reduce the opportunity for fraud and lead to reductions in the number of clerical staff in government departments.

However, there was an air of anti-climax in the Paymaster General's own office. Indeed, when the joint Paymasters George Rose and Lord Somerset took up their posts in 1804 they were horrified to find that no accounts had been submitted for audit to the Public Accounts Commissioners since Burke had left. Investigations revealed that the 'great arrears' in parts of the office were due not to general negligence on the part of the staff but to 'an immense increase of Business which could not be kept done in the ordinary Hours of Attendance'. We may guess that this was a direct product of almost continuous war against revolutionary France. Loyal co-operation from the staff enabled the arrears to be cleared on overtime, and following pressure from the joint Paymasters General the Treasury in 1805 approved proposals for extra staff, redistribution of duties, additional accommodation and salary increases 'to prevent the Business falling again into arrear'. To show that the staff must play their part also, the Paymasters issued a departmental minute urging 'much more punctual attendance' of the office juniors, the fixed hours being 11 am to 4 pm, six days a week.

Nor did Rose and Somerset's zeal end there. The discovery that the Secretary at War had been initiating payments without proper authority led to a sharp letter to the offending Minister, while a further revelation that an acting deputy paymaster in the West Indies had held over £5,000 of public money for five years (for two of which he was not in post) resulted in an immediate and searching examination of all deputy paymasters' accounts. It appears that no matter was too small for the Paymaster General's personal attention. The Minute Book of 1805, now in the Public Record Office, records the following letter to the head of the Stationery Office, signed by George Rose himself:

The Stationery supplied to this Office is of such Bad Qualities, especially the Pens, as to occasion much Inconvenience, and in the Instance of the latter very great Waste, as many are utterly useless and are thrown away. The Paymaster General will therefore be under a necessity of making Representation to the Treasury on the subject unless better articles are furnished.

The reply, if any, is not recorded.

In 1805 a further Paymaster General Act appeared on the statute books. This repeated many of the earlier provisions but changed others where previous Acts had proved inconvenient. For example, accounts were being delayed because of the remoteness of some outposts for which returns were required, and the Act provided that the accounts of stations beyond the Cape of Good Hope or Cape Horn should be kept separate, so as not to delay the finalisation of the rest. It also legislated for the missing accounts 1783-1804 to be drawn up as already demanded by the incoming Paymasters General.

In 1806 the office of the Treasurer of the Ordnance was 'regulated', and a year later came a further Act relating to the Treasurer of the Navy. This specified that he should draw money from the Bank only when it could be applied immediately to navy services; if he did not he could be forbidden to hold any further office under the Crown. Yet another Paymaster General Act followed in 1808, with even more detailed provisions for the preparation and audit of the office's accounts. The Act laid down definite rules on the method of operating the Paymaster General's account at the Bank of England; and provided for separate accounts to be maintained for half pay, Chelsea Hospital and pensions on the Compassionate List, for the annual accounts to be sent to the auditors within three months of the end of the year, and for a separate account to be made up for money paid by deputies on foreign stations. Once again the personal involvement of the Paymaster General is made clear, for the Act made specific provision for the transfer of moneys to his successor should he die, resign or be 'removed'. In 1808 also came an Act which provided for the Treasury to appoint Paymasters of Exchequer bills, which had been in existence since 1696 under the auspices of the Exchequer. The event is significant in the history of the PGO in that the duties of Paymasters of Exchequer Bills were taken over at the second major consolidation in 1848.

For 33 years after the departure of Burke in 1784 the paymastership was held jointly. The holders included William Wyndham Grenville and Frederick Robinson, who were later to become Prime Minister as Lord Grenville and Lord Goderich respectively. Generally it was a period when the Paymasters served honestly, quietly and without particular distinction. Meanwhile the Treasurers of the Navy included future premiers George Canning and Frederick Robinson, and a politician who is now best remembered for his witty plays, Richard Brinsley Sheridan, author of 'The Rivals' and 'The School for Scandal'. The redoubtable George Rose also held this office for 11 years from 1807.

In 1817 there occurred an event which may have appeared at the time to be of little consequence, but which with hindsight might be seen to anticipate the major consolidation to follow. For it was in this year, under Act of parliament, that the office of the Agent General for Volunteers and Local Militia was abolished, and its duties transferred to the offices of the Paymaster General and the Secretary at War. We may safely assume that this small-scale consolidation was a success; the fact is that it paved the way for the more substantial amalgamations of pay offices which created the Paymaster General's Office in 1836.

2. CONSOLIDATION: *Parnell's plan*

The Office is born

The PGO was born in an age of great reforms, a period when new and radical measures were rolling off the statute books almost as fast as parliament could enact them. It is hardly surprising that the amalgamation of four pay offices was overshadowed by more momentous contemporary achievements like the reform of parliament and local government, abolition of slavery, formation of police forces, introduction of the penny post and development of a national network of railways. Nevertheless, the 1836 consolidation was an important element in both the reform of government finance and the drive for economy in the public service. The results would have done credit to many an efficiency-conscious government of later years.

We owe the creation of the PGO to another Irish-born politician to make his mark in the British parliament: Sir Henry Parnell. A passionate supporter of reform in Ireland (he had opposed the Act of Union in 1800), Parnell was also a prominent civil engineer and a leading authority on public finance. In 1830, in a bound treatise 'On Financial Reform' which was to become a blueprint for government policy for upwards of 20 years, he first put forward the idea of amalgamating the pay offices, 'an entirely new principle for the management of all payments of public money'. It was, he said, the remedy for the existing evils such as inadequate accounting and security. It is not surprising that in the following year Sir Henry was appointed Chairman of the Commissioners of Public Accounts, a high-powered body which included the current Paymaster General of the Forces, Lord John Russell, and the First Lord of the Admiralty, Sir James Graham.

In their report on the Exchequer, which was to lead to radical reform in that department, the Commissioners promised a further report which would contain 'plans for the better payment of the public expenses'. Inexplicably this second report never appeared, but Parnell later confirmed that the intention was to recommend a single pay office for the armed services. A step in the right direction came in 1834, when the Paymaster General of the Forces took on the payment of half pay, pensions and allowances of the Commissariat, a government office making payments in the colonies. The path for Parnell's plan was finally cleared when in 1835, in recognition of his administrative ability and doubtless with consolidation in mind, Lord Melbourne appointed him to be the first person to hold simultaneously the four posts of Paymaster General of the Forces, Treasurer of the Navy, Treasurer of the Ordnance and Treasurer of Chelsea Hospital. Within weeks the Chancellor of the Exchequer had introduced a Bill to enable the duties of these offices to be combined in a single new department, to be styled **THE OFFICE OF HIS MAJESTY'S PAYMASTER GENERAL.** So logical and universally acceptable were its proposals that the Bill

William R.

Whereas by an Act passed in the 5th and 6th Years of Our Reign, entitled An Act for consolidating the Offices of Paymaster General, Paymaster and Treasurer of Chelsea Hospital, Treasurer of the Navy and Treasurer of the Ordnance, it is amongst other things enacted that it shall be lawful for Us, Our Heirs or Successors, by Warrant under the Royal Sign Manual, countersigned by the Lord High Treasurer or the Commissioners of the Treasury of the United Kingdom of Great Britain and Ireland, or any three or more of them, to abolish the said Offices of Receiver and Paymaster General of Our Guards, Garrisons and Land Forces, of Paymaster and Treasurer of all Monies for the maintenance or relief of disabled and superannuated Non-Commissioned Officers and Soldiers entertained in Our Royal Hospital near Chelsea, of Treasurer of Our Royal Navy, and of Treasurer of Our Ordnance, and in place of the said several Offices to constitute and appoint

One

Part of the KING'S WARRANT of 1836 setting up the PGO, including the signature of William IV.

passed through all its stages with neither discussion nor amendment. It became law on 25 August 1835.

More than a year was to pass before the PGO came into existence. It was a year of consultation between the Treasury, the service departments and of course Sir Henry Parnell, now inevitably designated the first Paymaster General. New procedures had to be devised, staff numbers and grades determined, and the problem of housing the new Office solved. Responsibility for all of these matters lay with the Treasury, and it was not until November 1836 that the final details were resolved. On 30 November, in the Brighton Royal Pavilion, William IV and Lord Melbourne at last put their signatures to the King's Warrant abolishing the existing pay offices and setting up the new Paymaster General's Office. The PGO opened for business the following day - 1 December 1836.

Headquarters was the former army pay office building in Whitehall, between the Admiralty and the Horse Guards. Of all the accommodation used by the abolished offices, this was the most convenient, being close to the Treasury, the Exchequer and the homes of the armed service departments. Some months before the consolidation the Paymaster General of the Forces had surrendered his adjacent official residence in exchange for a salary increase of £400 a year; this property was now converted to office use to enable the Whitehall building to house all headquarters staff.

On 1 December 1836 the establishment and pay scales were:

1 Assistant Paymaster General	*£1000 - £1100*
1 Accountant General	*£ 800 - £ 950*
1 assistant accountant	*£ 750 - £ 850*
1 paymaster, non-effective services	*£ 750 - £ 850*
1 paymaster, effective services	*£ 600 - £ 700*
1 cashier, Greenwich Hospital out-pensions	*£ 500 - £ 650*
8 principal clerks	*£ 450 - £ 550*
17 senior clerks	*£ 350 - £ 450*
29 assistant clerks	*£ 200 - £ 350*
1 assistant clerk, Sheerness	*£ 150*
32 junior clerks	*£ 80 - £ 180*
1 housekeeper	*£ 100*
1 head messenger/office keeper	*£ 100*
17 messengers	*£ 50 - £ 90*
112	

The staff number was 30 less than the combined complement of the former pay offices. The total staff cost of £30-35,000 a year represented a saving of nearly £11,000. The 112 personnel of the PGO were not all based at Whitehall, hence the large number of messengers. Seamen's wages and allowances were dispensed by full-time PGO employees at the major dockyards - Portsmouth, Devonport, Chatham and Sheerness - or by clerks sent periodically to the lesser yards of Woolwich and Deptford. Once a week a further clerk was dispatched to the Tower of London, to pay the wages of the ordnance. Chelsea out-pensions (those payable to ex-soldiers not resident at the Hospital) were paid by an Agent unconnected with the Office, but the seamen's Greenwich Hospital out-pensions were paid from a PGO outpost at Tower Hill. The new Office had also inherited small detachments in Dublin and Hanover, making ordnance payments in

Ireland and Germany respectively. In 1836 the Treasury had declared its intention of housing the consolidated Office 'under one and the same roof'. The reality was very far from the dream.

The staff of the new PGO were all transferees from the abolished pay offices. The merger gave rise to some discontent, for although no-one suffered a reduction in pay, many found that they were on a salary scale with a lower maximum than they could have expected in their previous departments. At this time the only course open to staff with a grievance was to submit a 'memorial' to their superiors, and 35 former employees of the navy pay office did just that, claiming their right to 'prospective advantages'. Parnell was sympathetic, but the plea was turned down by the Treasury. No-one, they said, had the right to be guaranteed prospective advantages.

The Whitehall office was arranged in four branches. One, under the supervision of the Assistant Paymaster General, was responsible for general establishment matters, and for conducting all correspondence. All letters, both in and out, were copied in longhand into large, bound registers, many of which are still available for inspection at the Public Record Office. A second branch, reporting to the Accountant General, examined the accounts and vouchers, and maintained the books. The other branches, under the two paymasters, actually made the payments, one handling those for 'effective' services (those which produced some kind of return, in the form either of service or goods) and the other the 'non-effective' payments, including half pay, pensions and gratuities. The PGO now had responsibility for making all payments in respect of the armed services, whether to staff, pensioners, contractors or other government offices. The departments determined the amounts and authorised them; the PGO obtained the money from the Bank and made sure that it was paid to the right person.

In the formative years of the PGO, the Treasury kept a tight control. It laid down the original establishment, regulations and accommodation. It also appointed all staff and authorised all promotions. Right from the start the Treasury Commissioners reserved to themselves the right to make appointments to the top three posts 'by selection, in or out of the Office, as they shall think most for the advantage of the public service'. In practice, the post of Assistant Paymaster General, the permanent head of the Office, was not offered to a promotee from within the PGO until 1935.

In Sir Henry Parnell, the Office had a political head who involved himself closely in both the work of the Office and the welfare of the staff. In 1840 he made a point of paying a personal visit to each of the port offices; the following year he finalised and issued a general minute which summarised the duties of every officer in the department and set out regulations on every aspect of the work, from the keeping of Accounts to hours of attendance. The Office was, after all, Sir Henry's own brainchild, and he was determined to make it a success. No grade escaped Parnell's attention in his quest for greater efficiency. At one end of the scale he secured the abolition of the posts of Accountant General and assistant accountant and their replacement by an accountant at only £600-£700 a year. By persuading the Treasury that effective and non-effective services could be conducted through the same account at the Bank, he combined the two paymasters in one post. At the other end of the establishment he dispensed with the services of the housekeeper, who had been responsible for supervising and paying the housemaids and charwomen, and transferred her duties to the office keeper with a pay rise of £20 a year. Farther afield, in 1837 Parnell secured from the War Office additional payments and pensions for the paymaster at Hanover and closed the Dublin office after moving its work to Whitehall.

From the outset the PGO had adopted double-entry book-keeping which, although still in its infancy in government accounting, quickly proved its worth in reducing the work of the clerks. Together with the measures already mentioned, it was instrumental in enabling Parnell to ask the Treasury in 1838 -just 15 months after the PGO's creation for authority to reduce the staff by 11. It was an offer which no Treasury could refuse: more than £4,000 a year was saved in salaries alone. The following year saw Parnell requesting a further reduction by five posts: this, too, was readily accepted. By now the PGO had 96 staff, of whom 52 were at Whitehall, 5 at Hanover, 21 at the ports and 18 at Tower Hill.

In 1841 the Whigs lost power when a no confidence motion was carried by just one vote. Sir Henry Parnell reluctantly departed from the Office as Baron Congleton, leaving a farewell message to the staff which praised them for their zeal, diligence and ability during a period of great changes and a minute to his successor listing further reforms which were still required 'in order to place the business of the Pay Office on a perfect footing'. Interestingly, one of these was the ideal of greater uniformity in the practices of the armed service departments, which is still not entirely achieved nearly 150 years later. A portrait of Sir Henry survives at the Wiltshire home of the present Lord Congleton: appropriately it depicts Parnell with his volume 'On Financial Reform', in which the idea of a unified pay office was first conceived.

Hanover

During Sir Edward Knatchbull's term, the little PGO outpost at Hanover briefly became the focus of attention. In 1842 the paymaster there was paying half pay and pensions to more than 2,000 officers (or their families) of the disbanded King's German Legion, a reminder of the age when Britain's Hanoverian monarchs still had an obligation to defend their European homeland. The claimants were paid in person, by post or through German banks, in foreign currency negotiated by the paymaster, John Taylor. Substantial profits were made on the exchange rates, some of which were passed on to the pensioners and the remainder retained to cover the expenses of keeping the office in Hanover.

In 1842 the gain by exchange of bills was £1,800, exceeding by nearly £500 the annual cost of maintaining the office and its staff of 1 paymaster and 4 clerks. However, Knatchbull was uneasy about the uncontrolled power enjoyed by the solitary paymaster, and quickly obtained Treasury authority to appoint a second person as joint paymaster (there were already joint paymasters at Portsmouth, Devonport and Chatham). The staff at Hanover became 2 paymasters and 2 clerks. Knatchbull's worst fears were confirmed within months, following a full investigation of John Taylor's accounts prior to 1842. Taylor had to confess to lining his own pockets with some of the profits which he had made on the exchange. He was discharged from duty and asked to repay no less than £7,000. Eventually the debt was cleared, but not before the disgraced paymaster had parted with every bit of his property in Britain and in Hanover, even to his household effects. An appeal to the Treasury failed, and two years after the Hanover affair burst into the records of the PGO Taylor died, a broken man, leaving a widow and eight young children. When the destitute Mrs Taylor pleaded for help the Treasury relented to the extent of a £36 a year pension, but only on account of her husband's pre-1836 service as a Board of Ordnance employee and translator of German.

Once more the Hanover office faded into the background of PGO history, emerging only when the declining pension numbers forced reductions in staff. Eventually it became no longer a viable proposition, and in 1862 it was closed.

Civil services

In 1841 PGO staff took over cash payment from the Bank clerks, and the post of Accountant was combined with that of Assistant Paymaster General. Four years later the Office absorbed the duties of the Agent of Chelsea Pensions, and with them another weekly commitment to send out a pay clerk with the necessary cash. 1846 saw one of the rare occasions when the PGO actually lost a block of work, when the payment of seamen's pensions was transferred to the War Office, and the outpost at Tower Hill was closed.

By 1848 the Whigs were again in government, under Lord John Russell, a former Paymaster General of the Forces and member of Parnell's 1831 Commission. The time had come to add civil payments to those of the armed services which the PGO had been dispensing so efficiently since the consolidation of 1836. In February 1848, the Treasury announced the intention to transfer to the PGO the duties of the two **PAYMASTERS OF EXCHEQUER BILLS.** A means of encouraging public investment in the national economy, Exchequer bills had been in existence since 1696. Originally they had been administered by officers of the Exchequer itself, but in 1831 Parnell's Commissioners of Public Accounts, in their report on the Exchequer, had recommended in no uncertain terms that 'the business of examining a claim to payment and of making that payment should be in distinct and separate hands'. As a result, under the Exchequer Act of 1834, the task of making payment on the bills had passed to the Treasury.

The Paymaster General in 1848, Thomas Babington Macaulay, was quick to disclose the Treasury's finding of six years earlier that the 10 staff of the Exchequer bills pay office were 'almost unoccupied for nine months of the year', and while claiming that his own clerks were never 'almost unoccupied', he noted that the Exchequer bills payments occurred at times of the year when the PGO work was at its lightest. Macaulay therefore supported the proposed transfer. It would, he said, 'promote accuracy as well as the dispatch of business'. It would save more than half of the cost of the Exchequer bills pay office and 'avoid those prolonged periods of cessation of duty, so injurious to the habits and efficiency of public servants'. By April 1848, well in advance of an enabling Act, the transfer of work was under way.

During the same month, the Select Committee on Miscellaneous Expenditure was considering the absorption by the PGO of the work of the **PAYMASTER OF CIVIL SERVICES.** Originally the civil service had been funded partly by fees and partly from the civil list. However, in 1830 responsibility for paying all civil service salaries and allowances had been transferred to the Exchequer, in return for the surrender by William IV of the hereditary revenues of the Crown. In 1834, the task of making payments had passed to the Paymaster of Civil Services at the Treasury, in accordance with the recommendations of the 1831 Commission.

The case for this further major consolidation was overwhelming. Charles Trevelyan, then an assistant secretary at the Treasury, declared that a pay office was 'an elaborate piece of official mechanism' which was 'capable of throwing off almost any quantity of work'. The Assistant Paymaster General (William Anderson) added that 'a few thousand additional accounts give no great additional trouble to those who have to superintend it because the business is conducted according to the fixed regulations which are applicable to a large as well as to a small number of payments'. The facts supported these contentions. The Paymaster of Civil Services employed 13 clerks to make 10,000 payments a year, while the PGO needed only 66 to pay several hundred thousands. Having listened to all the arguments, the Select Committee declared itself 'satisfied with the evidence as to the efficiency of the Paymaster General's Department'. It endorsed the proposed amalgamation with the Paymasters of Exchequer bills and of Civil Services, and went on to say that 'the machinery of this Department may be usefully and economically extended to many other Departments of the public service'. In particular the report named the Paymaster of Civil Services in Ireland as a likely candidate for merger: this eventually took place in 1861.

Thus on 14 August 1848 an Act was passed approving the second major consolidation. In December the Treasury issued a 163-paragraph minute detailing the procedures and the new establishment of the Office, which was:

1	*Assistant Paymaster General*	*£1000 - £1200*
3	*chief clerks*	*£ 550 - £ 700*
4	*principal clerks, at Chatham, Portsmouth, Devonport and Hanover*	*£ 450 - £ 550*
1	*book-keeper*	*£ 450 - £ 550*
13	*senior clerks*	*£ 350 - £ 450*
18	*assistant clerks*	*£ 200 - £ 350*
20	*junior clerks*	*£ 80 - £ 180*
1	*head messenger/office keeper*	*£ 150*
11	*messengers*	*£ 80 - £ 100*
72		

The total complement compared with the pre-1848 numbers of 82 at the PGO, 16 at the Paymaster of Civil Services and 10 at the Exchequer bills pay office. The overall salary cost was £19,900 a year.

In 1848 the proponents of consolidation had foreseen four main benefits, all of which were soon realised.

1. **A large reduction in cash balances.** By the nature of their duties, the Paymasters and Treasurers had to hold 'cash' balances at the Bank of England in order to make the payments when they were due. Amalgamation of the pay offices enabled the PGO to keep only one cash account with a considerably smaller overall balance from which payments for all services were made. The 1836 consolidation had effected a decrease in balances from £193,000 to £25,000, allowing the nation to earn £6,300 a year in interest on the undrawn funds. The merger of 1848 achieved even greater savings, for the Paymaster of Civil Services had maintained separate bank accounts for each of the services which he administered. The payments he made were only a quarter of those made by the PGO, yet the balances of £300,000 were 12 times greater.

SIR HENRY PARNELL, Paymaster General 1836-41, from a portrait by Samuel Lane.
Photo: Ken Bridle, 1984, by permission of Lord Congleton.

2. **Increased security of public money.** In 1872 the former Assistant Paymaster General, now Sir William Anderson, reported from his new seat in the Treasury finance division that in 35 years the sum of £1,400,000,000 had passed through the PGO's books. There had not been one case of internal fraud (he had conveniently forgotten the Hanover affair) and only £1,000 had been lost by fraud or forgery committed externally. In Anderson's view this confirmed the effectiveness of the unified checks employed in the Office.

3. **Increased convenience to public claimants.** Bankers and Agents benefitted considerably. Before the consolidations they had to send clerks to many different parts of London to collect their payments; now, they could present as many as 50 claims in a day to the Whitehall office and collect only one cheque in return.

4. **Saving of expense.** There were huge savings in establishment costs, particularly among the supervisory grades. Total numbers had been reduced from 168 (the complement of the separate offices before consolidation) to 72, although this would have been 90 had PGO retained the Greenwich out-pensions. The annual saving in salaries alone was £34,000, but there were many other gains. Office space was saved at Somerset House, the Tower of London, the Treasury and Chelsea Hospital; the official homes of the Paymaster General of the Forces and the Treasurer of the Navy were converted to office use; the three services paymasters had between them received £5,000, whereas the salary of the Paymaster General was fixed at £2,000 (he lost the £400 compensation for loss of official residence in 1848); and the nation even saved £99 a year by doing away with the Navy Treasurer's barge.

In short, for the nation and for the public, consolidation of the pay offices had been a Good Thing.

3. SURVIVAL : *under attack*

Monteagle

Seeing that the benefits of a unified pay office were so evident it is surprising that in the latter half of the 19th century the future of the infant PGO was in considerable doubt, as firstly its procedures and later its very existence were called into question by some of the leading politicians and officials of the day. These were years when the survival of the Office hung in the balance. The first assault came from the Comptroller General of the Exchequer, Lord Monteagle of Brandon. As Chancellor in 1835 this same gentleman had introduced the first consolidation Bill; in 1848 when the second amalgamation was proposed his was the only voice raised in dissent.

One of the main benefits of consolidation, the reduction of cash balances, was achieved by minimising the number of accounts at the Bank of England. Rather than keeping a separate bank account for each 'service', the PGO maintained aggregate accounts, which were topped up daily with sufficient funds to cover all expected payments. Although each payment was separately accounted for on the books of the PGO, to enable the Office to monitor the total spent from each service against the amounts voted by parliament, the basic practice of using the bank balances as a general all-purpose fund was continuously disputed by the Comptroller General.

In 1848 Monteagle had tried to amend the Consolidation Bill at its third reading and withdrew his clause only after the Duke of Wellington had persuaded him that his fears were imaginary. When the Treasury published the full details in a formal minute, Monteagle renewed his attack, asserting the 'entire illegality' of the PGO's practice. It was, he claimed, 'wholly at variance with the provisions of the Act regulating the Office, at variance with the provisions of the Appropriation Act, and of the constitution'. The Treasury minute was 'open to an interpretation subversive of all legal and constitutional checks'. All payments should pass through six stages of authorisation, including a warrant from the Comptroller General himself, before he would accept their legality. Faced with such censure the Treasury amended the minute to make it clear that no payment should be made for any service beyond the amount granted by parliament, and to reaffirm the Comptroller General's right to carry out checks on the issue of public money. Incredibly, these amendments pacified Monteagle, even though the Treasury continued to endorse the policy of keeping minimum cash balances and directed the PGO to apply to the civil services the systems of payment and account it was already operating for the armed services.

In 1854 the scent of war was again in the air, and with it the prospect of greatly increased payments from public funds. Now Monteagle was again at the PGO's throat. With highly-charged invective expressing his 'indescribable alarm' at the Office's 'deviations from the lawful practice', he penned a 12,000 word onslaught to Mr Gladstone (then Chancellor of the Exchequer), reciting all the old arguments about unconstitutional practices. This time he went too far, for his assertion that the balances in the Paymaster General's hands were 'indiscriminately applied to any purposes, whether legally sanctioned or not' was simply untrue. In a riposte of almost equal length, William Anderson (late of the PGO) exposed it as 'purely imaginary and totally incorrect'. He went on to claim that the Office could 'safely submit its accounts to the scrutiny of competent judges, in the full confidence that they will bear a favourable comparison with those of any public or private establishment in the kingdom'. To his chagrin Monteagle received no ruling of any kind from the Chancellor: the matter lay on the table until 1856.

In that year parliament set up a Select Committee on Public Monies which was to be concerned predominantly with the relationship between Monteagle's Exchequer and the PGO. The committee deliberated for over a year. Monteagle and Anderson between them gave evidence for 13 days. The document finally laid before parliament in 1857 consisted of some 450 pages of evidence and 27 appendices - in all, more than ¾ million words. At last the question mark attached to the PGO's cash balances was removed, as in general the committee declared themselves

> *satisfied, ... that the consolidation of the Pay Departments has been attended with public benefit; that it has diminished the balances left in the hands of the public accountants to the Crown; that it has increased the security of the public money; and that the regulation which requires the Paymaster General to make all his payments from a single cash balance has been attended with beneficial results.*

However, to maintain a tighter control on voted money, the committee recommended that the account for each service should be placed in credit monthly by obtaining supplies from the Exchequer, and that the Commissioners for Audit should be sent accounts showing the separate balances.

Interlude

There followed a period of 14 years' respite from the critics, but even in this brief interlude there was much activity within the department. In the early days of the PGO the wages of the navy were paid direct to the men by PGO staff stationed at the major dockyards, but in 1855 the payments were taken over by ships' paymasters, who in turn received the money from the PGO outstations. This proved to be a temporary phase, for in the following year the Admiralty appointed its own cashiers at Chatham, Devonport, Portsmouth and Woolwich, and the PGO offices were shut down. The Admiralty took on four of the messengers, but did not require the services of the clerks, nine of whom were pensioned off. The remainder were transferred to the Whitehall office, where work had increased due to expansion in the civil service and the additional payments generated by the costly Crimean war. The opportunity was taken to reorganise the Office into five branches, to be styled Army, Navy, Treasury (or Civil), Pay and Accounts (or Book-keeping). The grades and salaries of the staff were revised to bring them into line with those applying in the War Office and the Admiralty. Overall the establishment was reduced from 77 to 60, the lowest in the history of the Office.

In 1860 the redoubtable Mr Anderson, whose name recurs throughout the first 50 years of the PGO's existence, was appointed by the Treasury to look into the work of the Paymaster of Civil Services in Ireland, a Dublin office employing 20 staff. Inevitably Anderson recommended the consolidation of that Office with

GRANDFATHER CLOCK dated 1710, now in the Assistant Paymaster General's room at Crawley, but formerly at the Whitehall office.
Photo: Ken Bridle, 1985.

the PGO, a move which was implemented in 1861. Eight staff were transferred to the establishment of the PGO, four went to the Board of Works and the remaining eight posts were abolished. Once again the department found itself with an outpost in Dublin, which expanded briefly in 1864-73 when it handled also the work of the Office of Receiver of Constabulary in Ireland. Meanwhile, the office in Hanover was closed in 1862. The few pensions left were transferred first to foreign agents, and then to HM Consul.

In 1872 the Office took on the duties of the Accountant General of the High Court of Chancery in England, with no increase in complement. Between 1867 and 1877 the number of payments processed at the PGO almost doubled, as the Treasury implemented the phased monthly payment of salaries to civil servants. At that time salaries represented about a half of the payments made from the Office.

Vine

Charles Vine, a member of the Committee of Public Accounts and former Inspector of Audit, was the initiator in 1871 of a serious attack on the viability of the PGO. In a memorandum to the Chancellor of the Exchequer he contended that the justification for the Pay Office had been materially altered by the passing of the Exchequer and Audit Act of 1866. This required that accounts of all moneys voted in Supply for civil purposes should be forwarded direct to the

Audit Office by the PGO's government department customers, thus virtually eliminating the accounting responsibilities of the Paymaster General. The Pay Office, said Vine, was now merely a middleman between the departmental accountants and the Bank of England. It could be effectively abolished, with a considerable saving in manpower and no loss of security. He proposed that departments should draw their supplies direct from the Bank, that a clearing office should be set up at the Treasury to sort and schedule vouchers from the Bank, and that the cost of civil service pensions should be included in the effective service vote of each department rather than being grouped together as 'civil superannuation'.

Not surprisingly, the notion of abolishing the PGO did not find favour in every quarter. There were lengthy and sometimes acrimonious minutes between top officials, and on occasions the story broke into the national press. Vine found support in the Board of Trade, but fierce opposition from the army and navy, the Assistant Paymaster General (John Collier) and a former holder of that office, William Anderson, now Assistant Comptroller and Auditor, and KCB. The War Office succinctly and appropriately expressed the wish that the scheme be 'torpedoed'. The Chancellor of the Exchequer (Robert Lowe, Paymaster General 1855-8) had serious doubts, and officials at the Treasury were divided.

Another former Assistant Paymaster General now at the Treasury, Morgan Foster, maintained that the few staff who would be saved at the PGO would be more than offset by additional clerks at the other departments, extra costs would arise through the inevitable increase in cash balances, and the public would be inconvenienced through having to claim money in one place and collect it from another, instead of carrying out the whole process at the Pay Office. Sir William Anderson also spoke from experience. He had given nearly 50 years service in responsible positions at the Admiralty, PGO, Treasury and Audit department; he had also played a part in framing the Exchequer and Audit Act on which Vine's case rested. Anderson was able to state categorically that when the Act was drafted 'there was never the remotest intention of altering the functions of the Paymaster General', and went on to demolish Vine's argument that the abolition of the PGO would increase efficiency and save manpower. He countered the proposed amalgamation of superannuation and effective votes by restating that in 1831 Prime Minister Earl Grey had aggregated pension expenditure in order to 'better observe and control its growth'. So as to avert the criticism (which he levelled at Vine) of being out of touch with the proceedings of the Pay Office, Anderson went to the trouble of conducting his own investigation at the PGO before putting pen to paper. His findings were unequivocal:

> *Having completed my inquiry, I am bound to express my opinion that the business is safely and economically conducted, that the checks against irregularities and errors are complete, and that the manner in which the general duties of the office are performed is creditable to the public service.*

Anderson's paper stands on record as an authentic and invaluable synopsis of the purpose, history and importance of the PGO in the first 35 years of its existence. Such was its lasting value that 60 years later the Office ordered the printing of 125 copies, for future reference by the staff.

Smith

Before the issue could be resolved Charles Vine died in 1872. After three further years of indecision the Treasury announced that an inquiry into the duties of the PGO would be undertaken by William Henry Smith MP, Financial Secretary to the Treasury and the 'son' in the already established firm of London newsagents. W H Smith took another two years to come to the conclusion that the Vine proposals were impracticable. The change was too sweeping, he said, to be attempted without clearer proof that it would promote efficiency and economy. Nevertheless, Smith did agree with Vine that the effect of the Exchequer and Audit Act had been to convert the role of the PGO into that of a mere branch of the Bank of England. He recommended a closer look at possible manpower savings, the experimental removal of cash payment from the PGO to the Treasury and a regrading of much of the work to provide more clerks and fewer supervisors. The Treasury Lords approved most of Smith's recommendations, and sanctioned a further change in the following year. Until then, government servants who wished to receive their pay in cash were paid at their respective departments by PGO staff: in 1878 most departments took this task upon themselves.

The Office had not heard the last of W H Smith. In 1885 he put four questions to the Chancellor of the Exchequer which resurrected the subject of the Paymaster General's use of cash balances. This time a lengthy written reply seems to have laid the matter to rest once more. Shortly before that, Smith had been appointed by the Chancellor (Hugh Childers) to head yet another inquiry into the PGO's functions. This latest inquiry was actuated by a proposed expansion of the War Office and Admiralty which threatened to engulf the PGO building and force the Office to move elsewhere. The Exchequer and Audit Act, in its infancy when the Vine proposals were made, had now proved itself successful with the passage of time, and the long-serving Assistant Paymaster General, John Collier, had claimed retirement. All in all, it seemed a good time to reassess the value and purpose of the Office, and the number of people needed to carry out its tasks.

The Chancellor paid tribute to Sir William Anderson, 'that excellent public servant', whom he said had been instrumental in ensuring the efficient procedures. The concentration of previously scattered pay offices into one central department had proved to be one of the most effective reforms of the last half century. The compliments, however, were sugar on the pill, for Childers went on to claim that the reform had been 'so complete, and has so simplified the machinery of payment, as to prepare the way for a further reform which would render the maintenance of a separate Pay Office no longer necessary'. In other words, Smith had been appointed to do a hatchet job on the PGO. Nevertheless, Childers did stipulate that before recommending abolition the Treasury Lords would want to be sure that any clerks pensioned off in Whitehall would not be replaced by new staff elsewhere. They must also satisfy themselves that any monetary saving at the PGO would not be offset by additional charges for services rendered by the Bank of England.

The Smith committee met on five occasions, although Smith himself apparently visited the Office only once. They heard evidence from senior officials of the army, navy, Bank of England and PGO, including John Collier, who had been persuaded to defer his retirement for the duration of the inquiry but was excused ordinary attendance at the Office. The arguments centred mainly on the Office's effective payments, but inevitably its pension-paying role also came into question. The dice were loaded heavily against the PGO. The Chancellor had already let it be known that the idea of departments drawing directly from the

Bank was 'not unreasonable'. Even the Paymaster General, Lord Wolverton,who was a member of the committee, had expressed the view before the hearings began that the Office 'with propriety' could be abolished.

Therefore it came as no surprise when the committee recommended that the Bank of England should take on the effective payments, at an estimated cost of £3,000 a year. The PGO could then be abolished, for its other duties (ie pensions) could be transferred to 'some other Minister'. When Mr Collier retired the management of the Office would be placed under the direct control of the Treasury. Their Lordships agreed, John Collier was allowed to leave, and while the necessary legal formalities were being considered the responsibility for supervising the Office was entrusted to a chief clerk, Alfred Earnshaw.

From this point, just when it seemed that the PGO had reached the end of the line after only 50 years of service, the pressure for its abolition suddenly and mysteriously ran out of steam. Four years were to pass before the appearance of an Act giving the Treasury power to transfer the Office's functions to the Banks of England and Ireland, and even then there was no rush to use that power. The only notable change in procedures by 1890 was the absorption of PGO salaries into the Treasury vote. The valiant Mr Earnshaw was well over 78 by the time he was permitted to retire; his successor, Edward Vesey, held the fort as chief clerk until 1892, by which time he was nearly 72. In that year the Treasury formally acknowledged that the transfer of effective payments had been postponed, and a new Assistant Paymaster General, Charles Maude, was appointed.

Still there was no definite pronouncement as to the future of the Office. The effects were felt mostly at the lower levels, for although the chief clerk post disappeared with Mr Maude's appointment and two principal clerks were not replaced, it was the Treasury's policy during this period of indecision to promote people to vacant higher grade clerkships but to stop recruiting juniors. In 1887 there had been 17 second class clerks: by 1896 there were only four. The Office suffered also from a general reluctance to spend money on much needed heating and lighting improvements while the future of the Whitehall building was so uncertain.

At long last, in 1896, the Smith report was finally laid to rest. Due to altered circumstances, said the Treasury, the change was now unlikely to produce savings 'sufficient to outweigh the inconvenience which it would undoubtedly entail'. The plans to remove the Office from its Whitehall building had been scrapped; the number of senior officers had been reduced by natural wastage; and the number of effective payments had increased to such an extent that the Bank could no longer do the job for £3,000 a year. Thus the PGO was reprieved, but it did not escape change entirely. A wholesale reorganisation followed, which included the downgrading of effective work, the introduction of a new 'examiner' grade, and an overall reduction in the already depleted staff to reflect an increase in the working day to seven hours. The Office had survived the 19th century, but only just. As the age of Victoria drew to a close, the staff complement had dropped below 70, less than two thirds of whom were clerks. About 20,000 pensions were on the books, and around 400,000 payments were being made each year. Nearly £1 million was still being paid over the counter in cash.

The long years of uncertainty over, the PGO faced the future with some confidence. 1898 had seen the publication of a printed volume of instructions, a

'Memorandum on the Business of the Office', compiled by Frederick Bartlett (a young PGO clerk with a law degree) and published by the Stationery Office. In the following year the Office was given the task of paying an entirely new class of pensioners, the former teachers of elementary schools. No doubt it looked forward to a more secure future with an increase in business. It could never have foreseen the transformation which would be brought about by the Great War of 1914-18.

4. EXPANSION : *the Great War*

Impact

The dramatic impact of the First World War was felt in every aspect of the PGO's duties. Within the space of five years the little Office with its proud 80 years' tradition of accuracy and efficiency found itself with a 350 per cent increase in workload and an equivalent expansion in staff, most of whom had little or no experience of office work. In many respects the results of the war were permanent, for never again was the Office to revert to prewar levels of payments, pensions or staffing.

The long history of the PGO and its forerunners had prepared it to some extent for the effects of war. It knew from experience of the American, Napoleonic and Crimean wars that there would be a substantial increase in the number of payments for essential military and naval services. What it could not have expected was the scale of the extra work which would arise. For not only did the war effort necessitate the spending of vast sums of money on armaments, fuel and the pay and rations of the fighting forces: it also entailed the compulsory purchase of agricultural produce such as foodstuffs and sheep's wool, and an unprecedented expansion in the civil service, to staff new Ministries like those of Shipping and Munitions. All of these had to be paid from the PGO. The number of effective payments for army services which was 2,700 in the month of July 1914 (before the outbreak of war) increased to 10,000 by October and to 21,700 the following February. Navy payments rose from 5,800 to 15,000 a month in the same period. At the start of the war the Office was making about 700,000 payments (including non-effective) a year: when it ended in 1918 the annual volume had risen to 2½ million. By 1919 over £8 million was being paid over the counter in cash, by way of either imprest or direct payment.

The terrible casualties of the Great War also made their mark on the Office, which was already handling an increased rate of new superannuation to retired teachers and civil servants. Such was the intake of new awards of widows, dependants, wounds and disability pensions that the pension roll of the PGO climbed from 30,000 just before the war to 104,000 by the end of 1919. In addition there were thousands of gratuities to be paid to men who did not qualify for a pension. To make matters worse for the Office, this phenomenal increase in work coincided with a declining number of established staff. Although there was no conscription until the middle of 1916, such was the outburst of patriotic fervour occasioned by the outbreak of war and the accompanying propaganda, that from the outset men were queuing up - even lying about their age - for the opportunity to fight for their country. Before the war was 10 days old the Civil and Book-keeping branches of the PGO had lost seven of their 23 clerks, and many more were to follow. Four of them — John Bennie, James Davie, Thomas Phillips and Frederic Winter — were killed in action within the first two years of the conflict.

Only eight days after the declaration of war the Office approached the Treasury for temporary staff and overtime, to compensate for the loss of those who had joined up. As the increase in work added to the pressure caused by shortage of staff, requests for help were passed down the road to Treasury Chambers with monotonous regularity, and all of them were granted. There was little difficulty in recruiting temporary staff at 30 shillings a week; no doubt they saw their employment as all part of the war effort. Men applied for the work because they were either too young or too old to be taken into the forces, and for the first time in the department's history women clerks were employed, some of whom had voluntarily relinquished service below stairs while others had never known paid work at all. The growth of the civil service during the war was a matter of some concern to the government, which in 1918 appointed inspectors to investigate the work and staffing levels of every public department. At the PGO they found little scope for criticism, and could only conclude that 'having regard to the difficulties of accommodation and pressure of work' they were 'favourably impressed by the efficiency attained by the Department, and regarded both the numbers of staff and their rates of remuneration as reasonable'. At the time of the inspection the permanent staff of 55 male officers had dwindled to only 30-40, while the number of temporary clerks stood at 60.

However the real explosion in staff numbers occurred in the first year after the war's end, when the new pension awards were arriving at the rate of thousands each month. While Prime Minister David Lloyd George was demanding reductions in the size of the civil service and actually replacing departmental heads who failed to co-operate, the staffing of the PGO rose by leaps and bounds. By the time the war pensions had all been put into payment at the end of 1919, there were 240 on the payroll, compared with only 61 before the war.

Temporary huts

The 'difficulties of accommodation' reported by the inspectors in 1918 were most apparent in the room where payments were made, as they had been for the previous 50 years despite continual complaints by the Office and its customers. Some extra space was created in 1917 by taking in the private rooms of the office keeper (who was compensated at the rate of £50 a year) and in 1919 by the conversion to office use of the Horse Guards fodder store. By lucky coincidence the Board of Education decided at this point to pay English teachers' pensions themselves, thus creating further space for the new work. Nevertheless, by the middle of 1919 the staff employed by the PGO at Whitehall had grown from the pre-war figure of 50 to a grossly overcrowded 170. In 1918 the inspectors had found the building 'unsuitable for carrying on the present work of the Department'; the following year conditions had become intolerable, and even the Office of Works was moved to find a solution.

During the early stages of the war the lake in St James's Park had been drained to prevent its being used as a marker for bombing raids by the dreaded Zeppelin airships, and by 1919 both the lake and the Horse Guards Parade were covered in temporary huts accommodating the staff overflow from nearby government offices. The contraction, even disappearance, of many government departments soon after the war's end coincided nicely with the PGO's expansion, and so it was that as the Horse Guards huts were abandoned by their wartime tenants, the war pensions staff of the PGO moved in. By the end of 1920 the Office had taken over at least three of them.

36 WHITEHALL, headquarters of the PGO until 1940.
Photo: Ken Bridle, 1985.

Apart from the four who died on active service the department suffered no other fatal casualties in the Great War. Attacks by the Zeppelins and Gotha bombers, while striking terror into the hearts of Londoners then unaccustomed to aerial bombing, fortunately left the Whitehall office and its occupants unharmed. It is likely, however, that few staff escaped the loss of a loved one during the terrible conflict which claimed the lives of 750,000 Britons. For many years the Office would hold a tangible reminder of the horror of it all, in the shape of those packed registers of new war pension awards, each one the mark of someone's personal tragedy.

5. REORGANISATION : *between the wars*

Twenties

The end of the war heralded a general reassessment of the civil service which resulted in the birth of the Whitley system of staff/management consultation and the emergence of a new grade structure - administrative, executive and clerical. The need to assimilate the existing PGO classes into the new service-wide structure, and to acknowledge the permanence of the increased workload led to a major reorganisation in the Office, approved in 1920 but not implemented until two years later, by which time further additions were needed. Generally speaking the senior examiners became higher executive officers (HEO), the examiners were graded executive officer (EO) and the clerks became clerical officers (CO). However, the term 'examiner' persisted in the PGO until 1956. Many of the new staff were men who had passed the special 'Litton' examination for ex-servicemen, but some of those who failed or did not take it were retained as permanent, non-pensionable ('P' class) clerks, for many years after the reorganisation. Others were women, who had been taken on temporarily during the war and had now become established.

In 1922 the Dublin office, which had been virtually separate from the Whitehall headquarters since 1894, became a department of the new Irish Free State, but the PGO retained links with the Emerald Isle when at short notice it was asked to take on the payment of pensions to the disbanded Royal Irish Constabulary (RIC). Despite the obvious accommodation problems and the need to recruit a further 63 staff, the Office managed to commence payments only 24 days after the transfer was first mooted. By October 1924 the complement had risen to 281. The grades and pay scales were as follows:-

1	*Assistant Paymaster General*	*£1500*
3	*principal clerks*	*£750 -£850*
8	*heads of divisions*	*£550 - £700*
16	*senior examiners*	*£400 - £500*
44	*examiners*	*£300 - £400*
139	*clerical officers*	*£ 60 - £250*
1	*office keeper*	*£150 - £200*
2	*established messengers*	*£ 90 - £130*
43	*writing assistants*	*18s. 0d - £1.16s a week*
4	*typists*	*1s. 2d - £1.16s a week*
11	*unestablished messengers*	*1s. 7d - £1.12s a week*
1	*door and coal porter*	*1s. 7d - £1.12s a week*
8	*charwomen*	*15s. 6d a week*
281		

DARTMOUTH STREET, Westminster; No 1 Queen Anne's Gate Buildings (behind the van) was the branch office 1923-47.
Photo: Ken Bridle, 1985.

There also remained 38 temporary clerks, a number which reduced steadily as the post-war peak of pension work began to even out. The staff numbers were given a further boost in 1926, when 25 were transferred from the Board of Education to accompany the return of English teachers' pensions after an absence of seven years. Fortunately, by now the department had more permanent accommodation for the overspill from Whitehall.

Early in 1921 the Horse Guards Parade had been cleared of its temporary encampment, so that the Trooping the Colour ceremony could resume there after a few years in Hyde Park. The PGO 'hut people' had been rehoused in the Montagu House Bungalows on the Embankment behind Whitehall, but with the advent of the RIC pensions overcrowding again became acute. At last the Office of Works was able to offer more permanent accommodation, shared with the Passport Office in a new building in Dartmouth Street, near St James's Park station. From now on the Whitehall building would be referred to as 'main office' and No 1 Queen Anne's Gate Buildings as 'branch office', a function which it was to fulfil for the next 24 years. By 1928 the branch office itself had overflowed, and its filing section was around the corner at Caxton House West, in Tothill Street.

During and just after the war the Office had been preoccupied with processing a heavy workload in very difficult circumstances; by 1924 stability had returned, and the time was ripe for a fresh look at the department's working methods and practices. The impetus was provided by the appointment of a new Assistant Paymaster General. Roland Wilkins CB was a tall, forthright man with a classical education and long experience in the public service at both the Treasury and the Exchequer and Audit department. In his 11 year term of office at the PGO Wilkins never ceased to perform like the proverbial new broom. Pension clerks ceased their practice of writing simple replies on the backs of pensioners' letters and returning them to the sender: henceforth all correspondence was to be kept in pension files. Loose-leaf ledgers were introduced, to replace the bound volumes which had recorded what was in payment and to whom. To reduce the incidence of fraud, pensioners were now to be issued with handwritten vouchers which bore serial numbers, dates and amounts, rather than with blank forms. Declarations of entitlement were to be completed by pensioners annually instead of four times a year. Prompted by central government, the Office began to look critically at the use and design of printed forms, and at the retention periods of its records.

Above all, Wilkins was a great believer in delegation and accountability. Before his arrival the Assistant Paymaster General inspected all incoming correspondence, authorised every leave application, signed all typed letters (except those issued by the branch office) and endorsed each monthly account sent to a customer department. Within months of his appointment Wilkins delegated each of these responsibilities to either principal clerks or heads of divisions, though he continued to keep a close personal watch on the activities of the whole Office and came down hard on anyone guilty of the slightest error, particularly in arithmetical checking. In 1926 he reorganised the divisional structure of the Office numerically by functions. For example, the First Division (1D) dealt with establishments and office services, while 2D handled civil service salaries and superannuation and 3D examined the bankers' claims. From his arrival, Roland Wilkins showed a keen interest in the history of the department. Having appointed a young EO, Edmund Harwood, to be the first private secretary to an Assistant Paymaster General, he gave him the task of researching the origins of the Office from 1660 and organising the first exhibition on PGO history, which took place in 1927. Unfortunately Harwood's efforts were never published, but survive in the form of a typed manuscript.

During Wilkins's tenure of office there was only one change in procedures to have a substantial effect on the workload. Since the consolidation of 1836 the PGO had not only collected income tax from the salaries and pensions which it paid: it actually assessed the tax as well, so that there was much extra work when, as in 1916, a Finance Act introduced major changes in the tax structure. No doubt there was great relief when in 1928 and 1931 respectively the Office handed over to the Inland Revenue the tax assessment of both salaries and public service pensions. Four EO and 17 CO posts were transferred out at the same time.

Thirties

During the economically lean years of the 1930s jobs in the civil service were comparatively well paid, reasonably secure and pensionable, so they were highly prized by school leavers and other young people. When Birmingham lad Geoff Wheway passed the CO competition in 1938 at the age of 17 he readily gave up a job in his home town for a move to London, even though it meant paying £1 a week for 'digs' from a salary of £85 a year. However, because of the large numbers who had become established in the examinations immediately after the

Great War, there were few vacancies and recruitment by open competition was in some years suspended. In 1932 only 5 per cent of candidates for the CO examination achieved the inflated pass mark and six years later the acceptance rate was still only 20 per cent. The chances were no better for youngsters who took the simpler examination for clerical assistant (CA), a new grade which replaced that of writing assistant in 1936. Consequently the few young people who did enter the PGO in the 1930s were over-qualified for the menial, repetitive jobs which awaited them. They also found themselves greatly outnumbered by a generation born in the previous century who had quite a different outlook on life.

Promotions to the supervisory grades had almost come to a standstill. In the years between 1929 and 1935 only three men were promoted to EO and one to HEO. With such a dearth of vacancies management tended to pick men with special ability rather than mere seniority, to the dismay of many who had served up to 20 years in the same grade. Some of these had disability or illness which dated back to the war; others were disenchanted at the prospect of no promotion or even pay increment for the rest of their working lives. There was no wonder that their pace had slowed to such an extent that some of the youngsters could do the job in a third of the time. It was the same in the areas staffed by women. In the filing, detail and agreement sections, the younger girls would finish their work by 3 pm and occupy the rest of the day knitting, embroidering or making a dress to wear at the Office dinner and dance.

A feature of the work was the pronounced 'peaking', caused by the practice of paying all salaries and pensions (except teachers') on the last day of each month or quarter. This meant that examining staff were under pressure for 7-10 days of the month and slack for the remainder. Bank agreement staff always had to agree the banks' claims before they were allowed home, even if it took until 10 pm to find the last penny; yet on some days they were finished so quickly that they could play 'battleships' before the great charge for the main door at 5 pm.

There was also excessive formality, both in correspondence with pensioners, who were sent letters beginning 'I am directed by the Paymaster General to inform you' and ending 'Your obedient servant', and in the relationship between staff and managers. All EOs and above were called 'Mr' by their subordinates (there being no females of that rank): senior management addressed male staff by surnames only. High-ranking staff such as heads of divisions and principal clerks were encountered only if a serious error were committed, and very few staff saw the Assistant Paymaster General after their first day in the Office. Certain standards of dress had become traditional: when David Wheble joined the PGO as a CO in 1933 he was the only male in his division not to wear a hat to work — the others wore the conventional trilby or bowler. All men wore ties and suits (except on Saturday mornings when some dared to be seen in plus fours), and the ladies either dresses or skirts. The titles 'main office' and 'branch office' engendered feelings of superiority in the former and inferiority in the latter which encouraged the generally held view that only the lesser staff were posted to Dartmouth Street.

Despite all this, the young people who succeeded in entering the PGO towards the end of the 1930s carried out duties of appallingly poor quality with resolution, little complaint and faith in the future. They were grateful to have jobs and security: for these they were prepared to put up with the formality and the dinginess of life at Dartmouth Street and Whitehall.

6. WHITEHALL : *behind the green door*

Overcrowding

The building which served as headquarters for the PGO from its birth in 1836 until it was hit by a German bomb in 1940 stands on a part of the site of the medieval tiltyard belonging to the palace of Whitehall. The palace itself, used by the royal courts of the Tudors and Stuarts, was a sprawling collection of buildings between the Thames and the street now known as Whitehall. The tiltyard lay just across the road so that the jousting tournaments, bear-baiting, pageants and firework displays held there could be viewed from the vantage point of the palace windows. Beyond it stretched the green expanse of St James's Park. The tiltyard survived until just after the Restoration, when it yielded to the need for new buildings to house the Horse Guards and the palace housekeeper.

By 1676 the Paymaster General of the Forces had set up his house and office in a part of the Horse Guards building. In 1713 Sir Christopher Wren reported that the Paymaster had taken over accommodation in the north west corner originally intended as stabling for 30 horses, and soon it became clear that the army pay office needed a separate, purpose-built home. Under the direction of John Lane, Surveyor to the Horse Guards, work began in 1732 on a new building on the same site. The 18th century was a period of intense building activity in Whitehall. The Admiralty was erected to the north in 1723-6, and in 1750-8 the Horse Guards itself was rebuilt to the present design.

The new army pay office, which incorporated an official residence for the Paymaster General of the Forces and stables at ground level for the Guards' horses, was completed in 1733, at a cost of £3,842.10s.11d. It was a dignified, three-storey building with a brick frontage to Whitehall relieved by stone dressings and a large central gable in the pitched roof. The much plainer rear of the office overlooked an enclosed lawn to the Horse Guards parade ground. In 1806 the building was enlarged by the erection of a narrow, four-storey northern annexe on the site of a private house, to a design which harmonised well with the original building. Shortly before the consolidation of 1836 further office space was made available by the conversion of the rooms formerly used as the Paymaster General's residence, but the building retained official apartments for the office keeper and (until 1838) the housekeeper, whose presence on the premises was required at all hours. The whole office had about 40 rooms, lit by gas and heated by coal fires which in 1842 consumed about 120 tons of coal in a year. The interior contained many ornate features such as panelled walls, moulded cornices, cast-iron fireplaces and turned balusters on the wooden staircases. Despite all this, it is clear that soon after the second consolidation of 1848 the accommodation was proving to be unsatisfactory, for both staff and the visiting public.

Sir Charles Trevelyan reported in 1856 to a Select Committee on government buildings that the Whitehall office was 'totally unsuited' to its purpose, and in

36 WHITEHALL, decorated for the silver jubilee, 1935.
Photo: R C S Taylor's album.

1860 the Paymaster General (William Hutt) petitioned the Treasury with a graphic description of the worsening conditions:

> *During the busy period of the quarter the Office is filled with many hundred applicants for claims and a large space is required for their accommodation on the ground floor where the pay department is situated. In place of having ample room for this purpose there is only one small pay room with a back office which formerly was a kitchen and is lighted by gas. The consequence is that not only the pay rooms but all the surrounding passages are crowded to an excess with claimants of all classes such as General and other Officers, Widows of Officers, Bankers' Clerks, public servants, artificers, the allottees of sailors including their wives, relatives and others of a more doubtful character. These various classes are all mixed together in a mass so dense that on some days it is difficult to make one's way through them, and great delay arises from this cause in obtaining payment, an inconvenience which is much felt by bankers' clerks and men of business whose time is of value, and of which the general public make constant and loud complaints. The officers having charge of the payments are from the same cause much impeded in conducting their duties.*

Mr Hutt felt that the only alternative was to obtain the use of ground floor accommodation in a nearby building, in exchange for which he was prepared to release rooms on the upper floors of the office. By 1870 the pay room had been enlarged by taking in an adjoining room, but the volume of business and number of clerks had increased also, and the Paymaster General again complained that 'the greatest difficulty is suffered in maintaining anything like order in this part of the office'. This time he asked that an additional building be erected in the garden at the rear, and £650 was provided in the estimates. However the plan was aborted when the Admiralty and War Office announced their intention to expand on to the site of the PGO. The uncertainty created by this proposal was to blight all hope of improvement in the PGO accommodation for at least 25 years.

In 1882 the Assistant Paymaster General passed to the Office of Works a petition from the six clerks in the pay room:

> *The present room is almost uninhabitable. In winter the cold is intense and penetrating; in summer the absence of proper ventilation is almost unbearable. The room is on a level with the street and the absence of a basement floor or even cellarage renders it exceptionally damp and cold. The windows looking towards Whitehall are small and low. They at no time admit sufficient light and the dust and noise they do admit preclude the possibility of their being used for the purpose of ventilation. More than one of us have of late suffered from rheumatism and affections of the eyes from which we had previously been free.*

Again, nothing was done. It was, as usual, a time when the government was restricting public expenditure, and in any event the building was still under threat of demolition. In 1874 a fire occurred in the Whitehall office which revealed serious deficiencies in the emergency systems. The office keeper and coal porter were awarded gratuities of £5 and £3 respectively for their prompt action in putting it out, and a cistern, pipes and buckets were urgently obtained to safeguard the building during any recurrence. Five years after the fire, the Treasury approved the installation of extinguishers, but in the same week there was a blaze at the adjacent Admiralty building, in the course of which the PGO housemaids mysteriously lost their clothes and were later paid £5 in compensation.

Facelift

Bearing in mind the department's persistent difficulty in obtaining funds to carry out much-needed improvements, the events of 1910-12 were little short of extraordinary. It seems that one morning in 1910, Sir Charles Hobhouse, Financial Secretary to the Treasury, was walking to work when he noticed demolition works in progress on a large, stone-faced house at the corner of Great George Street, facing St James's Park and the entrance to Birdcage Walk. Reputed to have been the home of Judge Jeffreys and more recently of Sir John Aird, a leading building contractor, the house had a particularly fine façade which Hobhouse felt should be preserved. The solution, which he wasted no time in putting to the Office of Works, was to save the stonework and replace it on the rear of the PGO so that the latter would blend better with other buildings fronting the Horse Guards Parade. The matter was agreed between the Treasury and the Office of Works without prior consultation with the PGO, and the Treasury readily sanctioned the cost, which eventually totalled over £6,300.

For more than a year the Office was thrown into turmoil by the necessity to relocate the occupants of every west-facing room, for the west front had to be completely rebuilt in order to accommodate the façade of No 37 Great George Street. By 1912 the architectural style had been transformed. What was formerly a simple, Georgian exterior of brickwork incorporating 23 large windows was

HORSEGUARDS PARADE, showing (left) the west front of the PGO, behind the hedge.
Photo: Ken Bridle, 1984.

now a concoction of limestone blocks, arches and pilasters, in which the splendour of the stonework had clearly led to sacrifices in the amount of natural lighting. Even the little northern annexe was covered in limestone blocks, although it did escape internal changes. The only advantages to the PGO in this costly cosmetic facelift were that structural defects were discovered which could have caused problems in later years, and a new kitchen and refreshment room were provided in the attic rooms at third floor level.

In April 1919, the office was extended by taking in the ground floor fodder store, formerly the Horse Guards stables, which retained its brick-vaulted ceiling and stone floor while assuming the dignified title, 'Room 1'. It was modernised in 1931. After their brief spells in temporary huts and the Montagu House Bungalows, the war pensions divisions settled into the new branch office at Dartmouth Street in 1923. Very soon they were followed by the RIC and teachers' staff, so that the only non-effective work remaining at Whitehall was that of forces and civil service pensions.

The reactions of staff arriving at 36 Whitehall for the first time were mixed. Some found the exterior imposing, while others considered it plain and dirty. Some had difficulty in finding the building, until being told that they were standing in front of it; they had only to open the green door and they were in the PGO. When Roland Wilkins took up office in 1924, he complained at once to Sir Lionel Earle, head of the Office of Works, that both the eastern façade and the

1911 CORONATION PROCESSION of Their Majesties King George V and Queen Mary, from the windows of 36 Whitehall.
Photo: R C S Taylor's album.

entrance were 'dingy'. He asked for the stone facing to be steam cleaned and the entrance to be enlarged. Sir Lionel refused. Steam cleaning, he said, was often 'deleterious', and the entrance would not be altered because the existing appearance of the building was much admired both by himself and Sir Edwin Lutyens, the eminent architect, and designer of the Whitehall cenotaph. All that Wilkins managed to achieve was the redecoration of his own room and the installation of a genuine Georgian mantel over the fireplace. The admiration of Earle and Lutyens must have been shared by others, for after the building's appearance in the 'Survey of London' published in 1935 it was visited by several parties of antiquaries.

Cats and coronations

The luxurious accommodation enjoyed by the Paymaster General and the Assistant Paymaster General on the ground and first floors respectively, overlooking the Horse Guards Parade, contrasted sharply with conditions in the work rooms, which remained overcrowded, poorly lit, cold and often damp. Some of the rooms had very low ceilings, and those at the top of the building were reached only by steep, narrow staircases. To these problems were added the smell of manure from the Horse Guards when the contractor failed to empty the bins at the right time, and the inconvenience of fragments of the stuff being blown in through the windows from the yard below. Beneath the Office a bricked-up tunnel ran under Whitehall in the direction of the palace Banqueting House, and this gave access to an additional nuisance — mice. The department's remedy for this problem was to employ an Office cat, which succeeded in causing red faces at the PGO on at least two occasions. Late one evening in 1929 the poor creature went missing, and the nightwatchman telephoned Admiralty House next door to enquire its whereabouts, expecting to speak to the butler. Unfortunately the call went straight through to the bedroom of the First Lord's wife, who was none too amused by a late night enquiry about a ginger cat. Two days later Dame Caroline took the opportunity to put Mr Wilkins in the picture at a reception in the German Embassy and the unfortunate nightwatchman received a reprimand. In 1931 the office telephonist reported that his allowance for the cat of 2s.6d. a month (1d a day) left him out of pocket, and the Treasury Lords gave their grudging consent to increase the allowance to five shillings a month, not without comment that no other civil servant could expect a 100 per cent pay increase in the current economic climate.

The 47 open coal fires, generally lit only between October and April and refuelled by the door porter or messengers, generated little heat and frequent complaints from the staff. Apart from their inability to heat the whole of the larger rooms they had a tendency to fill the rooms with smoke when the wind was in a certain direction. When the Ministry of Works did get around to devising a comprehensive central heating system the war intervened and the project was abandoned. Even so, the machine girls enjoyed the days when they finished their work by three o'clock and met for a cosy chat around the fire, toasting buns and Welsh rarebit on old cake tin lids.

In a long, narrow room at the top of the building, 'Buz' Burwood, one of the Office COs, ran a much-praised luncheon club, assisted by a cook and a washer-up. During the peak work periods when staff were required to stay beyond normal hours to clear the daily bank agreement the restaurant served sixpenny (2½p) teas, consisting of poached egg on toast, bread, butter and a cup of tea. Sometimes, when there were any left after lunch, fish and chips were available too.

One feature of the Whitehall office which was unique among the many homes of the PGO was its fortunate position — between Horse Guards Parade and Whitehall — for watching London's pageantry. For the grand State occasions such as the 1937 coronation the front of the building was festooned with flags and banners, and committees were set up to decide the allocation of window space. In 1923 an Office instruction was issued forbidding staff from climbing on to the roof to watch a royal wedding procession. Weddings, funerals and the silver jubilee procession of 1935 all passed beneath the fascinated gaze of the PGO staff at 36 Whitehall, one of the most moving occasions being the funeral of the victims of the R101 airship disaster. Rehearsals for Trooping the Colour in Horse Guards Parade went on for many days before the event, and provided musical accompaniment for the mundane work of the Office: as the tempo of the military marches increased, so did the speed of the sorting processes. When the big day arrived staff were allowed to bring a guest or two to view the event from the upper rear windows. A stand was erected on the lawn of the office, and printed tickets were sold to the staff and their relatives.

The Whitehall office, partly destroyed by enemy action in 1940 and abandoned by the PGO, was patched up before the end of the war and taken over by the Admiralty. Subsequently the exterior of the ruined portion was rebuilt precisely to its former design, the only clue to the restoration being the slightly lighter colour of the replacement brickwork. Now modernised internally,

TROOPING THE COLOUR 1938, showing the PGO garden stand.
Reproduced by permission of Les and Marie Penn.

H.M. PAYMASTER GENERAL'S OFFICE

Trooping the Colour,

9th JUNE, 1937.

Row ....

No. ....

His Majesty's Birthday
(OFFICIAL CELEBRATION).

TROOPING THE COLOUR

WEDNESDAY, 9th JUNE, 1937.

Garden Stand, H.M. Paymaster General's Office, Whitehall, S.W.1.

Name of Holder ....

Row .... *Signature of Member of Staff* ....

No. ....

(Entrance by Whitehall only).

TICKET FOR THE GARDEN STAND, 1937.

it is the Office of the Parliamentary Counsel. Today No 36 Whitehall stands, as it has done for over 250 years, in the shadow of the dominating splendour of the Admiralty and Horse Guards, just a stone's throw from Trafalgar Square. Because of these imposing surroundings the old office rarely gets a second glance from passers-by; in any other setting it might be the centre of attraction and admiration. Few who pass its door can dream of the building's long history or of the drama of the day the bomb dropped in October 1940.

7. BLITZ : *a time of danger*

Outbreak of war

Towards the end of the 1930s growing international tension led to the creation of a government plan for the maintenance of public business and the protection of civil servants in the event of a war. In the PGO there was no doubt that a second world war would cause not just an increase in work and a lowering of staff experience as had been the case in the Great War: this time both the conduct of the daily business and the very lives of those staff who remained with the Office would be put at risk by enemy attacks from the air. The plan envisaged gas-tight rooms, bomb-proof shelters and the evacuation of many essential services from high-risk areas like London. At the PGO, training for gas attacks was being given to the staff as early as 1937, and rooms on the first floor of the Whitehall office were being converted into gas-tight refuges. By May 1939 these had been declared obsolete, and the emphasis had changed to protection from bombs and blast.

For the main office staff an air-raid shelter was erected in the Horse Guards Parade and shared with the Royal Army Medical Corps, while at the branch office the basement was specially reinforced to act as a shelter in the event of a raid. Wire mesh was fitted to the windows to protect them from blast, and male volunteers were recruited for air-raid precautions (ARP) and fire-watching. The paid pension vouchers, which had been stored for some years in a vault at nearby Storey's Gate, were moved to disused film studios at Elstree, Herts, to the great inconvenience of staff who needed to refer to them. Staff worked on overtime to prepare duplicate miniature ledger sheets, which also were sent to Elstree, as back-up in case the master ledgers were destroyed.

An ominous drain on staff resources, too, had begun long before the outbreak of war. Many departments concerned with the nation's defence, such as the Air Ministry, Ministry of Aircraft Production and Air Raid Precautions Department, expanded rapidly in 1938 and took staff on loan or transfer from other offices. Before the war began at least 10 experienced officers lost by the PGO in this way had been replaced by some of the few successful candidates from the 1939 open competition for COs.

Since the retirement of Roland Wilkins in 1935 the top seat of Assistant Paymaster General had been filled for the first time by a PGO product, James Mahood, but in 1938 he retired and another Treasury man took over. At the age of 59, Leonard Cuthbertson was to begin a seven-year term of unprecedented danger and difficulty for the Office. His first major task was to resolve the question: to evacuate or not to evacuate, should war break out. After a long and resolute fight against evacuation, because of the dislocation in government business which would result from separating the pay office from the spending departments, Mr Cuthbertson announced triumphantly in May 1939 that the Office would remain where it was 'unless circumstances compelled its removal

LEONARD CUTHBERTSON, Assistant Paymaster General 1938-45.
Photo: R C S Taylor's album.

elsewhere'. Certainly, he said, it would not be evacuated on the first alarm.

At the outbreak of war in the following September the government insisted on the preparation of firm plans to remove the whole Office (apart from a small nucleus) to the Lancashire resort of Lytham St Anne's. The scheme got as far as the requisition of three hotels for office accommodation, securing billets for the staff and labelling some of the goods to be moved, before finally being abandoned on the advice of the persuasive Mr Cuthbertson. The only PGO staff to be evacuated from London during the war were the five members of the Fourth Division who on 26 August 1939 accompanied the Bankers' Central Clearing House to Trentham Park Gardens, Stoke on Trent, and remained there until May 1946, making payments to the banks and sending on the vouchers by post to the PGO in London.

The war had no significant impact on the Office until it had been in progress for nearly a year. True, there were the predictable increases in effective payments and the intake of the first new war pensions, to disabled airmen and service widows, but the expected air raids did not materialise until September 1940 and most of the male staff were either too old for forces service or too young to be called up until later in the war. As the conscription net widened, some of the younger men volunteered before being called up, in order to have a choice of armed services, but the Office took rather a dim view of these volunteers. On occasions it actually refused to release them, and as a general rule would let staff go only a few weeks before they were due to be conscripted. While men were on active service the Office paid, to their bank or next of kin, the difference between their normal salary and service pay, unless they gained a commission. Sometimes the men called at the Office to collect this payment while on leave and were always welcomed by Mr Cuthbertson, but there was no regular system of communication between the PGO and its absent servicemen, and many overpayments arose because the salaries section was unaware of service pay rises. The Civil Service Clerical Association, the clerical staff's trade union, did attempt a periodic newsletter to some of its members whose whereabouts were known.

As work expanded and the younger clerks and examiners were called away the Office once more faced a problem of resources. It benefited from the June 1939 review of the CO competition results, when further candidates were declared successful, but from that point, examinations ceased until the end of hostilities. As in the Great War, the PGO was allocated temporary clerks recruited by the Treasury. Many were again women, with no previous office experience. Some of the established clerks received early promotion to replace examiners serving in the forces, to the dismay of clerks who were themselves on active service (although some were promoted *in absentia* later in the war). To reduce the need for additional staff most of the filing sections were closed down and the working day was extended. By May 1940 staff were working from 9 am to 5 pm, an increase of an hour a day on pre-war hours. Repeatedly Mr Cuthbertson rallied his staff with compliments on their achievements to date and appeals for even greater effort and sacrifice in the future. In some sections of the Office the accent was on maintaining fitness: physical exercises were introduced in some areas, while in others the managers encouraged a constitutional walk around the park just before the daily banking work arrived from Stoke on Trent.

In July 1940 came a warning from Prime Minister Winston Churchill to all forces and civil servants about the dangers of 'loose and ill-digested opinion' at a time of possible invasion or other form of battle for Britain's survival. The message was accompanied by a minute from the Assistant Paymaster General, urging that written submissions should show only conclusions and not lengthy reasons. He also asked for quicker action when decisions were made. In the early months of the war air-raid sirens would sound at the first sign of enemy aircraft approaching the Channel coast. The majority of day-time raiders never got as far as even the outskirts of London, and eventually it was realised that the general scurry to the Horse Guards shelter or the branch office basement was unnecessarily disruptive to the work. In 1940 an 'alert'system was introduced in government offices which gave warning of an imminent attack on London, and the staff were able to ignore other alarms.

In 1938 Dai Davies, then an HEO in the Whitehall office, had been detached from normal duties in order to organise air-raid precautions, and fire-watching duties began in both buildings from the outbreak of war. At Dartmouth Street fire-watching was shared with the Passport Office, the PGO representative being a head of division, John McIntyre. At first there was little activity to occupy the nightly volunteers, but when the blitz did begin their duties involved checking the roof and every room for incendiary bombs after each aerial attack. As a special favour to the fire-watchers the canteen in the main office would open at eight o'clock every morning for the serving of breakfast. The volunteers took what sleep they could, in order to perform their normal office duties after breakfast. Fire-watching gave some men the rare opportunity to enter the private dressing room of the Assistant Paymaster General, and even to make use of his personal toilet. On one occasion suspicion fell on the previous night's fire squad when the boss missed some sherry from his drinks cupboard: police detectives were called in but failed to find the culprit. In May 1940 an Office unit of the Local Defence Volunteers (later, Home Guard) was inaugurated: the 2nd City of London (Civil Service) Battalion, H Company, under the enthusiastic leadership of Captain Horace Fearn, an HEO who had to combine his new duties with those of senior examiner in 5D. The PGO's own 'Dad's Army' was entitled to wear uniform and to carry firearms, if necessary. The first delivery of rifles sparked off a nasty incident when observant but over-reactive troops on duty at the Admiralty stormed the Whitehall office brandishing revolvers and bayonets, and demanding to know the purpose of the newly-acquired weapons.

The blitz started in earnest on 7 September 1940. Damage to the lives and property of Londoners from direct bombing, blast and fires, was appalling. Marie Elliott, a CO in the branch office, was killed on her way home from work. Marie Hewitt (CA) and Percy Stewart (CO) were bombed in their own homes. Travelling to and from the Office became a hazardous business due to air raids at dawn and dusk. Each morning staff would leave for work not knowing when or even if they would arrive. Neither could they be certain that the Office would be there when they did.

The bomb

Tuesday 8 October 1940. After the clearance of early morning mist the sun broke through to promise a fine, cloudless day, as the PGO staff made their way to work for a nine o'clock start. By now disruptions to public transport were not unusual, so when Freddie Clay's tube train terminated its journey at South Kensington he accepted philosophically the prospect of a 2½ mile walk to Whitehall. Kathleen Kennerell alighted at Waterloo to see red 'alert' flags flying on Adastral House across the bridge: she took shelter until the raid was over. At 8.50 am, from a bus heading west along the Strand, Ray Heavens was aware of a solitary, low-flying aircraft flashing across the sky, unloading its deadly cargo of high-explosive bombs into the streets behind and ahead of his bus. Cyclist Geoff Wheway was already at work in the branch office when he heard the loud explosion from the direction of the PGO's main office. Walking across Trafalgar Square, Edna Long saw the bombs fall in the direction of Whitehall, only a few hundred yards ahead. By the time she had crossed the Square police had sealed off the road. They confirmed what she had feared: the PGO had received a direct hit. Edna ran on to her colleagues at Dartmouth Street to give them the terrible news.

Alan Lawrence was one of four PGO staff in a car which drew into Horse Guards Parade at 08.55. Hearing a shout as they parked, the men saw a messenger dash from the back door of the Office into the Admiralty building, and return with two marines carrying a stretcher. On passing through the Horse Guards arch they found the reason: the southern part of the Whitehall front had been reduced to a pile of rubble, spilling across the footpath into the street. Room 1 (the former fodder store), the rooms above it and the basement where staff sometimes sheltered in an air raid were all totally destroyed, and in the part of the building which still stood floors hung at crazy angles, unsupported at one end. The air was filled with dust and pension vouchers, and all around was confusion, heightened by the simultaneous bombing of three other buildings in close proximity. Philip Shingler had been on fire-watching duty, and was shaving in the first floor washroom when the explosion removed the floor beneath him, and he was left hanging from the wash basin. From the street, his predicament was spotted by Lance Corporal Rayson of the Military Police, on duty at the Horse Guards entrance. Rayson was on the wreckage before the dust had settled, freeing messenger Ernest Herring, who had been trapped by fallen masonry, getting a ladder up to rescue the plaster-covered Shingler, and going on to extricate a woman cleaner from the rubble, without a thought for his own safety. His bravery earned official commendation.

In minutes the London rescue services were on the scene to begin their grim search for survivors. Many had narrow escapes, and some were taken to hospital. Marion Pennelegion had fallen two floors, and certainly would have been buried but for the table which followed her down and protected her from flying debris. Soon the searchers found the barely identifiable body of Annie Lyon, a cleaner. It was to be several days before they recovered the bodies of Herbert Mason and Walter Sharpe, two of the 5D clerks whose workroom was totaly destroyed. Tragically, Mr Sharpe had been due to retire the previous week, but had volunteered to stay on for an extra 10 days to see the section over its busy period. Ray Heavens and others had begun to pull away the rubble covering a telephone kiosk outside the Office, knowing that it was sometimes used by passers-by as protection in an air raid, but they were stopped by deputy head of the Office Richard (RCS) Taylor in the interests of their own safety. Later the body of an Admiralty clerk was found behind the kiosk. The final toll of four dead and three injured could well have been much worse. At 8.50 am the building had been occupied by only the ARP and Home Guard duty men, the office cleaners, post-opening staff and a few other early starters: in another 20 minutes another 150 staff could have been at work.

When Freddie Clay arrived he managed to enter the building and get upstairs to don his Home Guard uniform and equip himself with a revolver. Crawling into the telephone exchange he found his colleague Tony Cansdale dealing with enquiries from pensioners, government offices and the relatives of staff. After parting with his tin hat to protect Cansdale from the falling masonry, Clay went off to salvage some of the Burroughs adding machines, an essential part of the office equipment. In his quest for a similar machine, Roy Halliday had roped himself to a colleague before crawling out along a bouncing, unsupported floor; hearing a gasp from the crowd below, Halliday looked back to find that his friend had released his hold of the rope. He just managed to get back to safety. Les Penn entered the building, too, to empty the huge, weighty Krupps safe, which had crashed to the ground from the first floor: he noticed that many of the fallen oak beams were eaten away by woodworm. Meanwhile, some of the branch office staff had arrived on the scene, and helped to sort through the rubble till evening.

Those who were not part of the rescue operation made their way to the garden at the rear of the building and thence into the Admiralty for a roll call; at length the decision was made to send the female and younger staff home and the rest to the branch office, awaiting further instructions. However the head of the banking division, William Corrock, decided that his work must carry on *al fresco*. While he took a taxi to the Bank of England to collect cash for the day's payments, others entered the building by a rear door to collect tables and chairs. Throughout the rest of the morning the overcoated Mr Corrock met the claims of banks and departmental imprest officers from his seat on the lawn behind the main office. Afterwards Kathleen Kennerell with two girls who had been inside the building when it was hit entered by the rear door and machined the daily agreement, incurring as they left a reprimand from Ministry of Works men attempting to make the structure safe. Next day three of the banks were to send

DESTRUCTION of part of the PGO building, 8 October 1940.

Reproduced by permission of the Trustees of the Imperial War Museum, London.

appreciative and congratulatory letters to the Office for continuing its business so efficiently in almost impossible circumstances.

Now Mr Cuthbertson had to make some important decisions urgently. The Whitehall building had been declared unsafe, and no offer of a long-term alternative was forthcoming. Once more he considered, but rejected, the idea of evacuation from London, and decided instead that the business would have to continue at Dartmouth Street, on the three floors already occupied by over 100 PGO staff. The remaining filing section there was closed, and next day its files were removed to the Stationery Office store at Cornwall House, near Waterloo station. What was left of the records of 5D (the division responsible for service retired pay) was transferred to Cornwall House also, together with the 5D staff, who had the unenviable task of salvage and reconstruction. The miniature ledger sheets were fetched from Elstree, but before much work could be done on them nearly all of the original ledgers were recovered from the wreckage, thanks to the sturdy binders which gave them protection.

The task of demolishing the unsafe parts of the main office was given to Mowlems, while some of the PGO staff volunteered to sift through the rubble as it was cleared, searching for files, ledgers and vouchers which could be taken to Cornwall House. They sought also missing personal articles, like bicycles, pens, cash collected for a presentation and the clothing of men who had changed into ARP or Home Guard uniform before the blast. Looting took place while the building was unattended: the kitchen officially lost £25 worth of stores, in addition to an unofficial cache of 'emergency' goods which had been destroyed in the basement. Among the losses were two oil lamps kindly loaned by Grindlays Bank to assist in the search — a cause of great embarrassment to the senior officers. There were also instances of PGO staff encroaching on the wreckage and impeding the demolition work — Mr Cuthbertson himself admitted privately to having rescued three calculating machines — and at one stage Mowlems threatened to down tools until they received an assurance that the interference would stop.

West Wing

Meanwhile the rest of the Whitehall staff, with their work, squeezed into the already crowded accommodation at Dartmouth Street, and resumed their business on 9 October. Once again the work was disrupted by air raids, which now were taken much more seriously. When the sirens sounded the lift was put out of operation, and valuable working time was lost as the staff descended up to five flights of stairs to the safety of the basement shelter. Some staff took their work with them, and continued to sort vouchers on a stretcher placed across their knees. Conditions at the branch office were so cramped that almost at once Mr Cuthbertson began to press for a more permanent solution, and on 25 October the lodgers from the main office were removed to the West Wing of Somerset House, at the northern end of Waterloo Bridge. The following January they were joined by 5D, who had suffered further misfortune at Cornwall House when an oil bomb caused more damage to their records.

The main office had moved into what was at the time of its erection and became again (many years after the war) one of the most splendid public buildings in London. Named after the Duke of Somerset whose former home stood on the site, it was begun in the 18th century to house a number of official bodies, including the Navy Office and the Royal Society. It was ironic that the

SOMERSET HOUSE, WEST WING, during the war, when it served as PGO main office.
Photo: R C S Taylor's album.

navy pay office had been situated at Somerset House before the PGO's 1836 consolidation. Built to line the edge of the Thames long before the construction of the Embankment, it is still best viewed from the river or Waterloo Bridge, to which it presents its long arcade of Portland stone. On its northern side, beyond an arched entrance from the Strand, lies a spacious courtyard enclosed by the East and West Wings, added in the 19th century. The West Wing, whose lower two floors were to be occupied by the main office, had been designed in 1853 by the eminent Victorian architect, Sir James Pennethorne.

If the PGO staff who moved to Somerset House in October 1940 failed to appreciate the history, romance and splendour of it all it was hardly surprising; for Somerset House, and more particularly the West Wing, had itself suffered bomb damage only weeks before, damage so bad that the Wing had been abandoned by the Estate Duty Office of the Inland Revenue. The rooms were huge, bare, cold and damp. Many of the windows were devoid of glass, so the central heating system was pitifully inadequate in the bitterly cold winter which followed. Fur coats and gloves were the working clothes of women staff unlucky enough to be posted there in 1940. There were open fireplaces, but no sign of any fuel. On particularly cold days some of the men would raid the deserted upper floors to break up some wooden furniture to get a fire going, and once on a fire patrol a pile of coal was found which was loaded into tin trunks and hauled into the draughtiest rooms for use in the bitterest spells. To make matters worse, the building was plagued by rats and mice, a nuisance for which the official remedy was the placing of sticky millboards on the floors as staff left in the evening, and disposal of the poor, trapped creatures the next day. When one girl left crusts in her desk drawer overnight she was aghast to find in it a nest of blind and naked new born mice in the morning. The West Wing was also dark, for blast-proof curtains had been fixed to those windows which were still glazed, and the low-wattage light bulbs were less than effective in the gloomy corridors.

Fire watching was essential at Somerset House, which had the potentially perfect trap for incendiary devices, in a stone balustrade surrounding the pitched roof and a clock tower which resembled the stonework but was, in fact, built of wood. At Christmas 1940 the rooftop volunteers witnessed a sea of flames on every side: it was a miracle that no further damage was done to such a prominent building. The Office paid men two shillings for a 24-hour shift of Sunday fire-watching, but refused offers of help from the female staff anxious to 'do their bit'. At Dartmouth Street one evening a PGO marksman managed to 'kill' a glowing 40-watt bulb in a building opposite. During the height of the blitz branch office staff were once evacuated to the park when a parachute bomb landed in a nearby tree. The Home Guard also continued its activities, finding the Somerset House quadrangle ideal for their regular drills.

Within the Office there was plenty of work arising from the growing numbers of effective payments at Somerset House, and the new war pensions coming into Dartmouth Street. The problems were exacerbated later in the war as women staff began to volunteer (and were released reluctantly) for service in the ATS, WRNS, WRAF or Nursing Reserve, and when extra work was imposed by new legislation such as Pay As You Earn income tax and the first Pensions Increase Act for 20 years, in 1944. In 1942 the working week was extended to 49 hours; although 'staggered hours' were allowed as a concession this meant merely that if staff wanted to leave at five o'clock they would have to work all day on Saturdays. Students from King's and Dulwich Colleges were taken on to assist in the pensions increase work, but the main support to the established staff who remained continued to come from temporary clerks who were at that time paid less than established clerks for doing the same work. Some of these incurred the resentment of the PGO regular staff because they failed to pull their weight, while others gave excellent service, went on to pass the reconstruction examinations after the war, and in some cases married young PGO warriors as they returned from the forces. A few of the temporary staff of doubtful reputation made a tidy profit from the sale of shirts and dresses to ration-prone staff.

By the end of 1942 the PGO had lost no fewer than 172 of its pre-war staff in 4½ years: 51 on active service, 68 on transfer or loan to other departments, and 53 through resignation, retirement or death. Each year, on the anniversary of the outbreak of war, the staff would gather in the shelters to listen to a broadcast service of prayer and rededication. Some gave up their annual leave to participate in a harvest camp organised by the Ministry of Agriculture and Fisheries.

The nightly air raids of 1940-1 were still imprinted on the minds of PGO staff when the news broke, at the beginning of 1944, of a new threat, from the pilotless flying bomb, V1. A secret plan, Operation Crossbow, was drawn up by the government for implementation in the event of prolonged attacks. It envisaged that most staff would be unable to get to work, and the business would have to be carried on by a very small nucleus of staff, resident at the office for

R C S TAYLOR, Assistant Paymaster General 1945-52.
Photo: R C S Taylor's album.

weeks at a time. They would be sustained by emergency 'Compo' packs, which it was claimed contained 'attractive items such as chocolates and cigarettes'. Home Guard chief Dai Davies was as sceptical as the PGO management about the chances of such attacks. If such a missile did appear in the sky, he predicted, the RAF would be on it like rooks on a crust. Nevertheless, the V1 attacks began in June and continued throughout the summer. The awful silence which followed the cut-out of a V1 engine before the weapon exploded as it hit the ground had a terrifying effect on some staff, who came close to nervous breakdown. Others had become hardened by the earlier blitz, and took the cool advice of the Assistant Paymaster General to take cover within the workroom rather than rushing outside to a shelter. The Crossbow proposals were not implemented, but instead the government once more raised the spectre of evacuation. The Office drew up a plan under protest, and was no doubt much relieved when the V1 onslaught suddenly ended in September 1944. In the following winter a fresh bombardment from the more powerful V2 rocket resumed the attempt to bring London to its knees, but oddly enough caused much less panic than the V1 attacks. Perhaps by then Londoners believed that the war would soon be over. Even so in the PGO 150 days compassionate leave were granted in 1944, for 77 separate incidents involving damage or destruction of the homes of staff members.

When the war ended in 1945, shortly after the retirement of the valiant Leonard Cuthbertson, the PGO pension roll had climbed to over 200,000, nearly twice the number at the end of the First World War. Six million payments a year were being processed, nearly three times the volume in 1918. The number of permanent and temporary staff on the payroll was nearly 500, of whom 70 were still either in the forces or with other departments. Three lives had been lost in the Whitehall bombing, three others had been killed in the blitz, and eight young men had died on active service. The eight were Percy Harden, aged 21, who died on 'Pioneer' service in Liverpool in 1941; Ronald Best and Thomas Mincher, both 20, killed in 1942; George Pearse (23) and Gerald Wheatland (21), in 1943; and John Sutton (21), Donald Marchant (22) and William Dennis (21), in 1944. All except George Pearse had joined the Office after the outbreak of war. Their names, with those who perished in the Great War, are remembered on a plaque which was unveiled by the Paymaster General in 1954 and which is now in the entrance hall of the PGO's Crawley Office.

The saga of the war years and the reaction of the PGO staff in the face of great adversity was summarised by the new Assistant Paymaster General, R C S Taylor, in a minute circulated to all staff. It ended with the following paragraph:

> *Looking back on the events we have all lived through, the Office has reason to be proud of the fact that on no occasion have we broken down and stopped payment. Even on the day that the Main Office was bombed the Paymaster and the Cashiers continued with their work amid dust and ruin. As Establishment Officer during the whole period I have been aware of the mounting difficulties experienced by one division or another and I have seen them overcome by the ability and decision of the senior officers coupled with the loyal support and untiring efforts of the remainder of the staff, including the Office Keeper and the Messengers. There has been danger at the Office, danger on the way to and from the Office and danger at home; but through it all the attendance has been beyond praise and it is due entirely to the courage, the resolute will and the public spirit of the whole staff that we have weathered the storm so successfully. Thank you.*

8. RECONSTRUCTION : *the post-war years*

Overflow

In common with the rest of the civil service, the PGO took several years to recover from the unsettling effects of the war. The increased workload - 50 per cent in the number of pensions and 100 per cent in the annual total of payments had come to stay, yet at the end of the war the department had no more established staff than in 1939, and 70 of those were still away from the Office. Not till August 1947 did the last war service recruit return to work; even then there were still 20 officers on loan to other departments, and until 1960 young men were called away to national service. The Office could not begin to release the 200 temporary staff engaged during the suspension of entry competitions, until the Treasury formally recognised the new workload by assigning extra established staff.

In October 1946 when more than half of the clerks and all of the typists were still 'temps', the establishment and pay scales were as follows:-

1 Assistant Paymaster General	*£1500*
1 Deputy Assistant Paymaster General (a new post, created in 1942)	*£1050 - £1200*
2 principal clerks	*£ 900 - £1050*
11 heads of divisions (SEO)	*£ 700 - £ 860*
30 senior examiners (HEO)	*£ 550 - £ 650*
1 staff officer	*£ 450 - £ 525*
9 clerks, higher grade — men	*£ 400 - £ 525*
— women	*£ 320 - £ 420*
67 examiners (EO) — men	*£ 150 - £ 525*
— women	*£ 150 - £ 420*
1 office keeper	*£ 230 - £ 310*
141 clerks (CO) — men	*£ 85 - £ 350*
— women	*£ 85 - £ 280*
190 temporary clerks	*variable rates*
4 established messengers	*£ 160 - £ 205*
13 unestablished messengers	*£2.12s.0d - £3.2s.0d a week*
10 temporary typists	*£2.6s.0d - £3.6s.0d a week*
10 clerical assistants	*£1.15s.6d -£3.15s.0d a week*
1 cleaner	*£1.10s.6d a week*
492	

Eventually a new complement was approved in which nearly all of the posts occupied by temporary staff were retained. Wartime acting promotions to the supervisory grades were then confirmed, service-wide reconstruction examinations were held for those deprived of the chance to become established during the war, and both open and limited competitions took place for younger folk

26 QUEEN ANNE'S GATE, Westminster, occupied by the PGO 1946-7.
Photo: Ken Bridle, 1984.

seeking a civil service career. Many of the PGO's temporary clerks passed the examinations and became permanent members of the Office. Between 1946 and 1949 no less than 177 COs and 12 CAs were recruited, posing an unprecedented training problem which was partially resolved by the appointment in 1949 of a staff training committee and by allocating training responsibilities to the new post of Controller of Office Services.

The staffing structure was not the only feature of the Office to need reconstruction. The intake of new war pensions which had led to the creation of two additional pension divisions soon stretched the branch office beyond its limited capacity, causing it to overflow into temporary accommodation in neighbouring streets. Clearly there was a need for a much larger building which could house the whole department permanently, but for about a year in 1946-7 the Office was spread between four different buildings. Establishments (1D), civil pensions (2D and 3D), bank agreement (4D) and forces retired pay (5D) were at Somerset House; English teachers (7D and 8D) and Second World War pensions (10D and 11D) were at No 1 Queen Anne's Gate Buildings, Dartmouth Street; Great War pensions (9D) were paid from Queen Anne's Chambers, Tothill Street; and the pensions of Scottish teachers and the RIC (6D) were at No 26 Queen Anne's Gate.

Of the three offices with a 'Queen Anne' connection, only 26 Queen Anne's Gate was built in the reign of that venerable monarch. Not only was it the oldest building ever occupied by the PGO: it was also the most picturesque and interesting. Backing on to Birdcage Walk and overlooking St James's Park, Queen Anne's Gate (formerly Queen Square) was erected in 1704 in a style of domestic architecture not long imported from Holland. It was a delightful little street of three-storey terraced houses of brown brick, decorated with stone bands between the storeys, dormers in the roof, sash windows and elegant timber canopies said to have been carved by naval craftsmen laid off from the dockyards. The number of blue, commemorative plaques on the walls of these houses confirm their desirability as residences for families of fashion and importance, especially in the 18th and 19th centuries.

The first occupant of No 26 was no less a person than the first Earl of Dartmouth (remembered in the street of that name). Between the wars it was the town house of the Marquis of Bute, and when taken over in 1946 by the 26 staff of the Sixth Division it still possessed bells to summon the servants; Dickensian kitchens extending under the street; a creaking, two-person lift that must have been one of the earliest to be fitted in a private house; and an oak staircase whose spiral, decorated balusters were so highly valued that the Ministry of Works had to encase them for protection during the PGO occupation. The Scottish teachers' staff had their office in the children's bedrooms right at the top of the house, behind the dormer windows; during the harsh winter of 1946/7 they enjoyed the comfort of hand-basins and open coal fires. The whole of Queen Anne's Gate remains attractive and well-preserved to this day, although some of the buildings, including No 26, have acquired an extra storey. No 26, which stands opposite a contemporary statue of Queen Anne herself, is now the office of the Girls' Public Day School Trust.

Much less romantic was the accommodation in Queen Anne's Chambers, opposite the southern end of Dartmouth Street, which the Ninth Division occupied for only a few months in 1946. A seven-storey office block incorporating the shops in Tothill Street and Broadway, it is now the home of HM Procurator General and Treasury Solicitor, and various parliamentary agents and solicitors. Two archways between the shops still bear the inscription 'Queen Anne's Chambers'.

Meanwhile, the original branch office was nearing the end of its shared tenancy with the Passport Office. Unlike 6D's pretty little house around the corner, the red-brick, eight-storey office in narrow Dartmouth Street is remembered with little affection by the people who worked in it during and after the war. True, it had features unknown in the Whitehall office, such as large, open-plan rooms, central heating and an electrically operated lift to all floors, but despite its impressive, tiled entrance hall, PGO staff remember it as a squalid, dusty and impersonal place. The branch office workrooms on three of the upper floors had rows of ceiling-high filing cabinets (running along the joists because of the weakness of the floors) and a counter at each level where clerks could attend to visiting pensioners. At the top of the building was a somewhat spartan canteen where, in the gloomy days of food rationing, the speciality was dripping toast. It was not surprising that many preferred the delights of the nearby 'Two Chairmen'. Dartmouth Street seemed to breed its own brand of eccentricity, like the head of division who habitually paraded in his silk dressing gown and bedroom slippers after a night's fire-watching, the senior examiner who boiled fish in the tea urn and used to spit into the street from his fifth floor window, and the staff and pensioners who kept the office supplied with black market tea and silk stockings. The old branch office still stands in Dartmouth Street; now styled 'Expro House', it is in 1985 the office of Esso Exploration and Production UK.

Russell Square

Throughout 1946 the Assistant Paymaster General and the Ministry of Works scoured the more respectable parts of the west end to find more permanent accommodation. After a fruitless search in Mayfair and Kensington Mr Taylor finally announced in December that within the next month the branch office staff at Dartmouth Street and Queen Anne's Chambers would be moved to a modern office on the north side of Russell Square, Bloomsbury. The news was greeted with mixed feelings, for despite the squalour and discomfort of their current premises, the staff did find them convenient for the Southern Railway, Underground, Army and Navy Stores and their lunchtime stroll by the lake in leafy St James's Park. By comparison Russell Square was situated inconveniently, and although it did possess a fine, tree-sheltered open space for those disposed to commune with nature, there were no ducks within a half-hour walk.

The second largest of London's fashionable squares, Russell Square had been developed in 1800 as the principal feature in a huge estate owned by the Duke of Bedford, from whose family tree derived the street names Bedford, Gordon, Russell, Tavistock, Torrington and Woburn. The central open space had been laid out originally by Humphry Repton, the notable landscape gardener, but had been altered substantially in the early 1960s. In the 20th century Bloomsbury had become the 'village' of artists and show-business personalities, many of whom were spotted by observant PGO employees. It also had the British Museum, the University of London, and a motley collection of offices large and small, and hotels good and bad.

The PGO was destined for an eight-storey corner building of red brick, faced with stone on the lower two floors and harmonising remarkably well with the style of much older buildings around the Square. It had been designed as part of a hotel complex, but on its completion in 1941 it was requisitioned by the government for use as a hostel for American servicemen and later as headquarters for the new Ministry of Information. When first occupied by the PGO, Russell Square House still had a somewhat unfinished appearance, because of its blank western wall. It was not until 1955 that the staff witnessed the building of a contiguous office block in identical style, to be let to the Ministry of Health. When the PGO began to move in it shared the building with the Ministry of Labour, Customs and Excise and United Nations Organisation, but like a cuckoo in the nest it soon set about having the other tenants removed in order to create space for itself. As room became available, in August 1947 the Sixth Division were dragged unwillingly from their self-contained snugness at Queen Anne's Gate and in March 1948 5D were transferred from Somerset House; eight months later the civil superannuation division followed them; and by September 1949 when the rest of the Office arrived the PGO was under one roof for the first time in its history. It had taken 113 years to fulfil the Treasury's objective so hopefully expressed in 1836.

Russell Square House had one thing in common with both Whitehall and

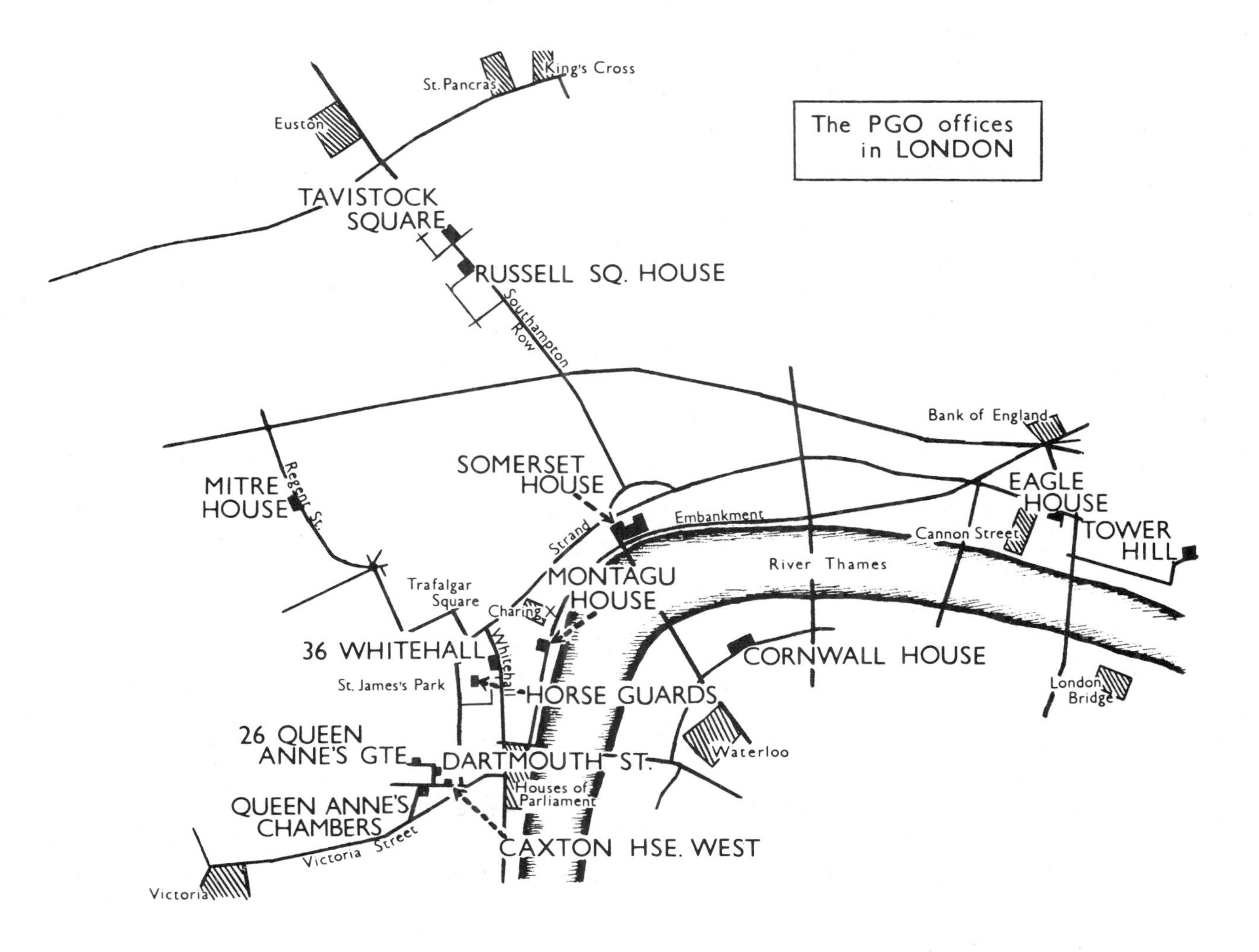
The PGO offices
in LONDON
Euston
St. Pancras
King's Cross
TAVISTOCK
SQUARE
RUSSELL SQ. HOUSE
Southampton
Row
Bank of England
MITRE
HOUSE
Regent St.
SOMERSET
HOUSE
Embankment
Strand
EAGLE
HOUSE
Cannon Street
TOWER
HILL
River Thames
Trafalgar
Square
Charing X
MONTAGU
HOUSE
36 WHITEHALL
Whitehall
CORNWALL HOUSE
St. James's Park
HORSE GUARDS
London
Bridge
26 QUEEN
ANNE'S GTE
DARTMOUTH ST.
Waterloo
Houses of
Parliament
QUEEN ANNE'S
CHAMBERS
Victoria Street
CAXTON HSE. WEST
Victoria

RUSSELL SQUARE HOUSE, Bloomsbury, occupied by the PGO 1947-71.
Photo: Les Penn, 1958.

Somerset House; it had a heating problem. Many of the metal-framed windows had been damaged by blast and were ill-fitting, while the coal-fired central heating system proved woefully inadequate to warm such a large building. In the extremely cold first winter of 1946/7 the unfortunate staff were forced to wear overcoats and gloves; their morale and efficiency were further impaired by having to work by candle-light when ice-bound colliers could not reach the Thames-side power stations. Continuous complaints to the Ministry of Works resulted in some promises of improvement in the heating, but little action apart from some supplementary heaters for the notoriously cold seventh floor, and eventually an admission in 1952 that the heating system in Russell Square House was the worst that they had ever had to deal with.

The early years in the new building showed no let-up in the volume of work or in the frequency of new legislation. The 1944 Pensions Increase Act was followed by others in 1947, 1952 and 1956, each one containing new features and requiring considerable clerical effort. In 1948 the Office acquired another new class of pensioners, the former employees of the new National Health Service, who merited the creation of a Twelfth Division and became the fastest growing of all the PGO's pension services. Despite a succession of organisation and methods studies by Treasury officials, each new block of work was accompanied by an increase in staff, for very few of the department's processes had been mechanised. In 1952, for example, the Pensions Increase Act necessitated the addition of 7 EOs and 13 COs. Two years later, when a Ministry of Food deficiency payment scheme threatened an extra four million payments, approval was given for a further 57 staff.

This proved to be the last straw which once more caused the department to look around for accommodation for a branch office, for Russell Square House was now in the sole occupation of the PGO, and full to capacity. The lot fell to the 46 staff of the Tenth Division, now handling disability retired pay for servicemen of both wars, to leave the fold for pastures new. In the summer of 1954 they moved south-west to the top of Mitre House, part of a 1920s office complex above the stores of busy Regent Street. Staff who worked there recall that during the day the building would throb to the beat of the Edmundo Ros Latin American band, rehearsing in the Coconut Grove nightclub in the basement, while in the evenings, after a spell of overtime, they would exit through an archway of palms erected over the door to attract the customers. In 1985 the basement is a Middle-eastern restaurant.

When the short-term tenancy of Mitre House ended early in 1957 the Office declined an offer of premises in Marsham Street, Westminster, because it knew of suitable space available just around the corner from the main office, in Tavistock Square. By now 10D had been selected as guinea pigs for the first mechanisation of pension payment, so its presence was required in Russell Square House, close to the machines and the watchful eye of senior management. So it was the Fifth Division (army and navy retired pay) which moved into rooms in an office block similar in age and style to the main office, and unpretentiously called '1-6 Tavistock Square'. Thanks to the success of mechanisation in containing the growth of the clerical staff there was no demand for more office space while the department remained in London. The only changes were the exchange of 11D (weekly-paid pensions) for 5D in 1959 when it became the Fifth Division's turn to be mechanised, and the transfer to Tavistock Square of the newly-formed Computer Group (CG) in 1964.

New blood

In 1956 the Treasury, of which the PGO was still a sub-department, had a problem. The retirement as Assistant Paymaster General of Alfred May (who had succeeded R C S Taylor in 1952) had left the Office with no suitable candidate to fill the vacancy, for the next three most senior PGO men were all over 60. After leaving the post vacant for nearly three months in 1955 they had appointed Cyril West from the Ministry of Agriculture, Fisheries and Food, but sadly Mr West died from cancer within a year of taking up his post, and once again a solution had to be found.

For some time the Treasury had been concerned about the 'age block' of senior officers in the PGO which was obstructing the promotion of eligible young people to higher positions and which would undoubtedly cause difficulties when

MITRE HOUSE, Regent Street, partially occupied by the PGO 1954-7; the entrance is just left of the lamppost.
Photo: Ken Bridle, 1984.

the senior men all retired within a few years of one another. At the end of 1955 the youngest officer of SEO rank or above was 54; the other 16 had all been born in the 19th century. Only three of the 30 HEOs were under 40. The Treasury were worried also by PGO's frequent requests for additional staff and accommodation. They had only just received an estimate that 47 more staff would be needed if teachers' pensions were to be paid monthly instead of quarterly. Mechanisation, recommended in an organisation and methods review of 1955, was probably the answer, but it would need firm leadership if the entrenched attitudes of long-established managers were to be overcome. The PGO badly needed to be modernised, and it required an injection of new, younger blood at the top. The man the Treasury chose was John Hamilton Vetch, one of their own principals. At 45, he was the youngest man ever to head the PGO. He was given a promotion to assistant secretary and five years in which to drag the Office into the 20th century.

John Vetch had only once visited the PGO previously, and that was to investigate the claim for more staff to handle the proposed monthly payment of teachers' pensions. Consequently his arrival was greated with reserve by some of the longer serving staff, but many were soon won over and co-operated in the introduction of a management style which to them was little short of revolutionary. With only a few years to achieve his goal, Mr Vetch wasted no time in getting to know his staff. He interviewed every HEO, every EO and

1-6 TAVISTOCK SQUARE, Bloomsbury, partially occupied by the PGO 1957-66.
Photo: Ken Bridle, 1984.

many of the clerical staff too. He discussed their careers, their jobs and their aspirations. None of his predecessors had attempted such a thing, which impressed the staff concerned but did little to allay the resentment of the older managers. The interviews soon confirmed that procedures in the PGO were old-fashioned and rigid, and that the remoteness of managers from their staff was making for low morale and inefficiency. A detailed examination of correspondence from pensioners and the draft replies sent for typing revealed out-dated phraseology and an arms-length relationship with pensioners, although Mr West had accepted a Staff Side suggestion to adopt a 'Dear Sir ..... Yours faithfully' style of letter and had for the first time allowed EOs to sign.

So John Vetch began his own campaign of reconstruction which embraced better management/staff relationships, simplification of procedures and the elimination of waste. He co-operated in the transfer out of the Office of some of the brighter young men whose careers were being blocked, and imported through the Treasury Pool promotees who brought new blood and fresh experience to the Office. He persuaded customer departments to adopt more standardised accounting methods; regraded some of the effective CO work to CA; authorised the suspension of returns for other departments until such time as they were missed and called for; abandoned the notion of last penny accounting; abolished the 'reading off' of paid pension vouchers; instituted regular weeding of files to economise on space; edited letters to pensioners to prompt a more direct and personalised style of drafting; imposed standard abbreviations for postal addresses; urged staff to encourage pensioners to claim money due to them; introduced the payment of pensions direct to bank accounts without evidence of life; and ended the payment of cash to other departments. He also renamed the divisions to indicate more clearly the nature of their work, and so were born the titles EOD (Establishment Officer's division), FD (finance division), MD (mechanised division), and the pension divisions CS (civil service), NHS (National Health Service), RP (retired pay), TP (teachers' pensions) and WP (weekly paid). An important prerequisite for mechanisation of pensions was the decision to stagger payment dates throughout each month and thereby avoid staffing for the end-of-month peak of work.

The reforming zeal of John Vetch was almost brought to an untimely end in the appalling Lewisham train disaster of 1957. In dense fog one evening in early December he was travelling home in the rear carriage of a crowded commuter train when it was struck from behind by the steam express to Ramsgate. The express continued to plough into the electric train, which had stopped at a signal, forcing the rear carriage into the air and demolishing a bridge over which a third train was about to pass. Miraculously, despite injuries to the leg and head, Mr Vetch was able to escape by scrambling from a window, and made his way home to Hayes. Nearly 100 people were killed in the accident, including Staff Side member Leonard Ambrose, a 38 year old EO in 8D.

Rush hour travel was ever one of the more unpleasant aspects of working in London. It was one reason why many civil servants were to welcome the prospect of escape from the rat race, offered by the government dispersal plans of 1962-3.

9. EXODUS : *a new home in Sussex*

Decisions

Since the 1939-45 war, despite an often brief tenure of office and the more pressing demands of other Ministerial duties, most Paymasters General have managed at least one visit to see the PGO at work and to meet some of its staff. By 1962 the machinery producing pension payments was working efficiently, if rather loudly, and no doubt it was with pride and satisfaction that in September John Vetch escorted on the customary tour of the Office the newly-appointed Paymaster General and Chief Secretary to the Treasury, John Boyd-Carpenter. All had gone smoothly and according to plan until Mr Vetch was bidding farewell to his guest at the front door. It was then that the Minister dropped his bombshell. 'Vetch', he said, 'is there any reason why your department should not move out of London?'

In his capacity of Chief Secretary, the Minister had special responsibility for planning the relocation of London offices, a major plank of government policy. However, this was the first intimation that the PGO might be a serious candidate for dispersal; yet it was no great surprise that as Paymaster General, Boyd-Carpenter might wish the PGO to lead the way. The advisability and practicality of moving a whole department into the provinces had to be weighed very carefully. Mr Vetch and the senior colleagues in whom he confided could not deny that some of the pension work could be done outside London, with the important proviso that it needed to be close to the machinery on which its efficiency depended. The banking work, however, must remain within an hour's journey of London, in order to process payments inside the 'recourse' period allowed by the banks, and even then it would be necessary for a small clearing office of the PGO to remain in the City where banks could present their claims daily and receive payment without delay. Moreover, the computer system now being planned would automate a large part of both the banking and pensions work, so it would be crucial for the staff concerned to be close to the new computer. The staffing problems which dispersal would create would be substantial but not insurmountable. The biggest one would be a dilution of experience caused by a traumatic changeover of personnel; about two thirds of the existing staff might be lost to the Office because they were either unwilling or unable to move their homes. If the new location were to be within the home counties, however, some people might be prepared to commute to work and so reduce the drain on experience.

Following the Minister's initial approaches to the PGO and other departments, Sir Gilbert Flemming was appointed to review the case of every government office in London, and to recommend which should be moved out. The Flemming report, issued in May 1963, proposed the dispersal of some 18,000 posts, of which 10,000 were in the Post Office Savings Bank, Civil Service Commission, Ministry of Public Buildings and Works, and the PGO.

The proposals for the PGO did not find favour in the Office, for while Sir Gilbert had recognised the need for a City clearing office and for banking work to be within easy reach of London, he concluded that the pension divisions (some 400 staff) did not need to remain near London at all. He proposed that they be dispersed to the north of England. Fortunately, John Vetch was able to persuade both the Treasury and the Minister of the importance of keeping the banking and pensions work together in one place, and in July 1963 he was able to announce to the staff the government's decision to move the whole of the PGO to a place within an hour's journey of London, except for the small 'caller' office to be set up in the City. The staff accepted the news philosophically, and were eager to help select the location.

The Minister had earlier raised the possibility of a dockyard town. Because Portsmouth was too distant, he suggested Chatham, with the New Towns as a feasible alternative. Mr Vetch had extolled the virtues of Brighton. In August a 'long list' of 12 locations was drawn up by the Departmental Whitley Council (DWC) and submitted to the Ministries of Works and of Housing for their comments. The choices were Bishops Stortford, Brighton, Chatham, Colchester, Crawley, Guildford, Harlow, Maidstone, Redhill/Reigate, Stevenage, Tonbridge/Tunbridge Wells and Woking. In the light of the Ministries' views on planning considerations and availability of housing for the staff, a short list of five emerged: Brighton, Chatham, Crawley, Harlow and Stevenage. In September 1963 all members of the staff were asked to vote for three of them, in order of preference. The results were as follows:

	First choice only	***All three choices***
Brighton	*184*	*297*
Chatham	*37*	*131*
Crawley	*55*	*267*
Harlow	*39*	*104*
Stevenage	*54*	*146*

Soon afterwards, however, Brighton and Chatham eliminated themselves because neither could supply houses to rent, leaving only the three New Towns, each of which had said that they would welcome the PGO. After transferring the votes of those who had given Brighton or Chatham as their first choice, Crawley emerged as a clear winner:

Crawley	*171*
Harlow	*46*
Stevenage	*70*

In December 1963 the choice of Crawley was endorsed by both the Paymaster General and the Staff Side of the DWC. In discussions the Office had expressed a preference for an empty site adjoining Crawley station, but when this was refused because it had been earmarked for possible shops, car parking or other offices, the only viable alternative was accepted — an undeveloped area in Haslett Avenue, between Three Bridges station and the swimming pool. Although this decision was made in May 1964, the time taken for the Ministry of Public Buildings and Works to design the building, obtain planning permission,

SITE OF THE PGO, cleared for building, August 1966.
Photo: Geoff Wheway.

invite tenders and select a contractor (Richard Costain), plus a six-month government freeze on office building, meant that the first sod was not cut until July 1966. The building operation was scheduled to take two years. In the meantime, the Office looked around for temporary accommodation for advance parties of staff.

A condition of the New Town Commission's acceptance of the PGO in Crawley was that the housing requirement would be spread over a period of years. This coincided with both the Office's wish to reduce the impact of the expected staff turnover by phasing it over several years, and the needs of the staff themselves, some of whom wanted an early move to Crawley while others wished to stay in London as long as possible. As soon as the location was decided, therefore, the Office established the likely needs of its employees. Some were unable to leave London because of family ties; some preferred to take the opportunity to transfer to other departments; some lived in the Crawley area already and were delighted at the prospect of working near home; some lived south of the Thames and were prepared to commute to the Office to avoid the disruption of moving house. Others, however, were happy to seize the chance of obtaining better living accommodation in a pleasant corner of the south-east, and were ready to take advantage of dispersal terms which included payment of removal expenses, travelling expenses and excess rent allowances.

TEMPORARY HOMES OF THE PGO in Crawley
Top: OLD POST OFFICE
Bottom: GOFFS PARK HOUSE

Top: SUSSEX HOUSE
Bottom: DRILL HALL.

Photos: Ken Bridle, 1984-5.

Buildings

While personal decisions of this kind were being made, the Treasury was writing to all government departments to seek head for head exchanges for the PGO folk who did not wish to move to Crawley. The choice of location proved to be a popular one, for the applications far outnumbered the vacancies. The exchanges began in the summer of 1964 and continued until 1968, by which time more than 200 had taken place. At the same time the Office was recruiting new entrants from the Crawley area to replace staff who retired or resigned before dispersal. Thus the Office was faced with an ever-growing number of staff anxious for their work to move to Crawley as soon as possible. Between 1964 and 1967 the PGO secured the temporary use of four buildings in order to phase the exodus from London.

The first to be occupied was a building in the High Street which had been originally the town's post office and later its public library. Later the lease was obtained of Goffs Park House, an isolated council-owned mansion in beautiful parkland; next came two floors of Sussex House, a seven-storey modern office block above the Starlight Ballroom and bowling alley complex; and finally the former Drill Hall of the then disbanded Territorial Army, in Kilnmead. The temporary offices are remembered with affection by all who worked in them, such was the informal atmosphere and community spirit which they engendered. Three of them were also convenient to the amenities of the town centre, while at Goffs Park the staff enjoyed idyllic surroundings complete with squirrels and a placid lake, hot meals prepared on site and surplus bedding plants by courtesy of the resident park-keeper. All four buildings were linked by a delivery service operated on pedal cycle by a messenger whose other duties included stoking the boilers at the Old Post Office.

The planning of interdivisional staff moves and removals between offices resembled that of a military operation. CS2 division was the most affected, suffering four changes of building and one of floors (in Sussex House) in the space of only five years. The scale of the dispersal exercise may be gauged from the following chronicle of events:

October 1964 — March 1965	CS2 and TP2	Russell Square	→ Old Post Office
July 1965	CS2	Old Post Office	→ Goffs Park
	TP1	Russell Square	→ Old Post Office
August 1965	CG	Tavistock Square	→ Russell Square
December 1965	CS1 (part)	Russell Square	→ Goffs Park
September 1966	CS1 (part) & CS2	Goffs Park	→ Sussex House
	CS1 (remainder)	Russell Square	→ Sussex House
	NHS	Russell Square	→ Goffs Park
October 1966	EOD (part) & CG (part)	Russell Square	→ Goffs Park
	WP	Tavistock Square	→ Russell Square

May 1967	CG (part) CG (part)	Goffs Park Russell Square	→ Drill Hall → Drill Hall
June — August 1967	RP2	Russell Square	→ Drill Hall
August 1967	CG (part) CG (remainder)	Drill Hall Russell Square	→ Haslett Avenue → Haslett Avenue
December 1967	EOD (part) EOD (remainder)	Goffs Park Russell Square	→ Sussex House → Sussex House
July 1968	CS1, CS2, EOD	Sussex House	→ Haslett Avenue
August 1968	WP & RP1 NHS RP2 TP1 & TP2	Russell Square Goffs Park Drill Hall Old Post Office	→ Haslett Avenue → Haslett Avenue → Haslett Avenue → Haslett Avenue

While the workforce began to muster around the centre of Old Crawley the site for the new purpose-built office and computer hall was being prepared in a lush meadow near the railway line, more than a mile to the east. In 1966 there was no square-about and no Russell Way, which was completed just before full occupation of the new building and named from the PGO's association with Russell Square in London. Access to the site was direct from Haslett Avenue, through the camp of builders' huts. In one of these were held weekly progress meetings between representatives of the Ministry of Public Buildings and Works, their consultants, the contractor and the PGO. Gradually the five-storey concrete monster began to rise from the open spaces of Three Bridges, despite the sort of unforeseen problems which always seem to dog building work.

One of the works supervisors was a man who could not abide heights. On one occasion, after being pushed and pulled up a vertical ladder (before the construction of stairs) the poor man finally cracked when expected to walk along some narrow girders at the top of the building and was in such a panic to get back to safety that he ran straight across a floor of wet cement. Another early (and recurring) problem was the periodic flooding of the central courtyard and the lift shafts, caused by a stream which had always run through the site and clearly intended to continue. In the link block connecting the computer hall to the main office a pipe duct along one side was found to be blocked by dead field mice; in a duct on the opposite side were dead house mice. When workmen lifted the pipe between the two they were knocked back by the stench of corpses, the result of a mortal battle between opposing armies. Despite such difficulties, however, the work proceeded according to schedule, with special emphasis on completing the single-storey computer hall and link block by July 1967, in time for delivery of the new computer hardware. In the event the hall was finished on time, but the computer did not arrive until nearly a year later.

However, the completion of the link block made further office space available. This was taken up by the CG systems and programming teams — the first occupants of the Haslett Avenue building. Working in the middle of a

NEARING COMPLETION: the PGO in May 1967.
Reproduced by permission of the Property Services Agency, Department of the Environment.

construction site was not without its problems, the worst of these being the notorious Sussex mud which they had to negotiate, knee-high in wellington boots between the unsurfaced car park and the office door. Tea was provided from the builders' huts, but there were no other refreshment facilities. With another outpost to serve, the messenger exchanged his trusty bicycle for a minibus, which not only carried documents between the offices but also ferried the CG colonists into town for shopping or lunch at the Post Office canteen.

In July 1968, right on schedule, the rest of the building was ready for occupation. It had 127,000 square feet of floor space within four sides of a square with a 'well' in the middle. Among the innovative features were a 'roll store' consisting of mobile shelving for the retention of obsolete vouchers and files, a document hoist, four passenger lifts to all floors, a spacious staff restaurant with bar, and special rooms for rest and recreation. One by one, the divisions moved in from their temporary homes and from Russell Square. Tavistock Square had been abandoned to other government users in October 1966, to the relief of CG and WP who had suffered for two years from refuse smells and cooking odours in a badly-ventilated building. The weekend removals to Haslett Avenue proceeded without a hitch, apart from a strike on the day that TP were moving from the Old Post Office. The men were aggrieved because a new foreman refused them breakfast money, and were appeased only after the Office parted with a £5 handout.

Because of the late delivery of the computer, pension work continued to be sent to Russell Square for processing on the old machinery for another two years, and it was October 1971 before the last of the banking work was computerised. FD's book-keeping section was the last contingent to move to Crawley, in

September 1970, because the services of MD and FD2 (the division processing payable orders manually) were not required once the new computer was 'live'. In November 1971, when the five-person caller office was established in the City at Eagle House, Cannon Street, the PGO was able to say farewell to Russell Square after 25 years. It is ironic that in both Russell Square House and 1-6 Tavistock Square (now 'Tavis House') the space vacated by the PGO on dispersal to the provinces was taken up by other departments which not only stayed but expanded in London.

First impressions of the £¾ million Haslett Avenue building (named Sutherland House in 1978 after the Duke of Sutherland, Paymaster General in 1925-8), were of almost clinical newness, brightness and cleanliness, in comparison with its predecessors. The floors were vinyl-tiled, the walls emulsioned and the brand new filing cupboards, desks and chairs a delicate shade of battleship grey (the cupboards were resprayed in more interesting colours some years later). However, even this glass palace was not without its problems, chief among which was the inability of the oil-fired heating system to cope with the cooling effects of large metal-framed windows. In addition, the delivery of oil created noise and smell before the construction of a more remote terminal, and the steam output from the computer's air-conditioning plant caused many a false alarm for the local fire brigade. Internally, the valuable walnut-cased grandfather clock built in 1710, one of the few pieces of furniture to be brought to Crawley from Russell Square, had to have its top decor removed in order to fit beneath the low ceiling of the Assistant Paymaster General's room.

Settling in

So the dispersal exercise ended. It had been a major feat of planning and consultation, which earned honours for many of those most closely involved, including Establishment Officer Freddie Clay, who had overall responsibility for personnel matters throughout. Between 1964 and 1970 the Office had lost 272 staff by transfer to other departments, most of them in return for incoming transferees, although there were no exchanges for the staff of MD and FD2 who left towards the end. By 1970 the Office had dispersed, transferred or recruited locally about 700 staff to the new building, a massive task for its small personnel and training sections. Yet it was a proud boast that no-one had been forced to move to Crawley, and everyone who did not want to be dispersed was taken into other departments with the sole exception of eight machinists.

There are few people today who doubt the wisdom of the PGO's dispersal. The staff who moved home from the London area were spared often long and tiring journeys by public transport, arrived at the Office in a fitter state for work, and were able to spend more time at home. True to its word, Crawley did welcome the PGO; the Office as an employer, the new residents and the many sports teams quickly became accepted and established in the community. The injection of new blood and experience from other departments more than compensated for the experience lost, while the recruitment of new staff proved much easier in the New Town. The move also facilitated the employment of part-time staff and others with domestic commitments. Within the Office the existence of a luncheon club and bar, and the creation of new social and sports clubs, helped to reawaken the community spirit which had been lacking in the PGO for many years. Dress became more informal: for the first time males were seen in coloured shirts and females in trousers. Few would dispute Mr Vetch's

TOPPING OUT ceremony on the roof of the PGO, 23 May 1967. Shovelling cement is John Vetch (Assistant Paymaster General) and behind his right ear is Freddie Clay (Establishment Officer).
Reproduced by permission of the Property Services Agency, Department of the Environment.

contention that the Office had become 'undoubtedly a better and brighter place'.

Paymaster General towards the end of the dispersal exercise was Viscount Eccles, who even today recalls the 'good attitude' which prevailed at Crawley. He admits to early doubts about the relocation programme, founded upon the traditional reluctance of the British to uproot or undergo change. Nevertheless, after his first visit to the PGO in its new home he came away reassured by the success of the move and impressed by the feeling that here was an office in which people enjoyed working.

John Vetch had taken his appointment in 1956 on the understanding that he could take up a 'return ticket' to the Treasury after about five years in post. Having achieved much of the modernisation and mechanisation he had desired, he was thinking of using that ticket when the Office was hit by what he later called the 'thunderbolt' of dispersal. Although invited back by the Treasury shortly afterwards he had acquired such affection for the PGO that he determined to stay on to steer the Office through its latest crisis. Even after dispersal there came three more trauma which needed his leadership: the Pensions (Increase) Bill 1971, which established two-yearly reviews; decimalisation, which required not only considerable changes to office forms and the computer systems but also wholesale staff training; and, in the winter of 1970/1, the Post Office strike.

When Mr Vetch retired in 1971 after 15 years as permanent head of the Office, he had served under nine different Ministers, and had held the post longer than any of his predecessors with only one exception. He was to be succeeded by four Assistant Paymasters General who were all PGO products — Freddie Clay, the first ever to rise to the top of the Office from humble beginnings as a CO; Norman Norfolk, pioneer of mechanisation and computerisation in the PGO; Eric Webster, architect of personnel planning in the dispersal exercise; and Laurie Andrews, the first Assistant Paymaster General to have entered the Office after the war.

Under their leadership, the removal from London has been accompanied by a gradual separation from the apron strings of the Treasury, symbolised by the creation of a separate PGO Administration vote in 1978. Nevertheless, like all other departments, the Office has been under increasing scrutiny and pressure from successive governments to review expenditure and personnel management policy. A major step in the progress towards independence occurred in 1969 when a small Staff Survey Unit (SSU) was set up to carry out internal, but independent, staff inspections and reviews of organisation and methods. Previously such studies had been the prerogative of the Treasury. In its first five years the SSU investigated the work of all eight pension divisions as well as some of the non-pension areas. Its findings led to radical changes in many long-standing practices. In particular, much of the checking which had been a feature of the PGO since its creation was eliminated or downgraded, manually-entered ledger sheets were abolished, and electronic calculators were introduced to replace salary tables. The unit also took steps to ensure that jobs were more satisfying and productive. In pension sections EOs became mainly managers of staff rather than checkers; CAs were employed in every section for the first time; some of the more complex tasks such as the calculation of pensions increase and of the effect of re-employment on pensions were spread around rather than being carried out on a few elite sections; and the number of pensions administered by a section was increased from about 6,000 to nearly 10,000. Middle management posts were reduced, and RP and TP became two divisions instead of four.

Renamed Management Services (MS) in 1976, the unit has since reviewed every post in the department apart from those of senior rank which are still inspected occasionally by the Treasury. The implementation in 1979-80 of a more sophisticated computer pension system enabled MS to recommend further increases in section caseloads, to 12-18,000, depending on the complexity and variety of the work in each division. Thus, with the aid of computerisation and other technology, the unit helped the PGO to arrest the habitual growth in staff numbers and to reduce administrative costs.

Arising from early recommendations by the SSU, in 1972 the Office set up its own Internal Audit team to carry out independent audit appraisals and tests throughout the department, formed a Checking (later, Financial Control and Security) Committee in 1974 to determine and review the extent of checking, and in 1975 instituted quality control, to monitor the effects of changes in the checking levels.

Because of the value and importance of the new computer equipment, custodians were employed from the outset to guard the building after working hours. The increasing security risk to government offices caused the introduction of pass cards in 1973 and the appointment of a security officer the following year. While the building was still under construction there was some panic in the local police force one evening when three Irishmen alighted from a train at Crawley and asked for directions to the PGO; however, it turned out that they wanted only a job on the building site. On another night a custodian had the shock of his life when at 2 am he heard a noise outside and looked up to find a face with large, staring eyes at the window. Too terrified to go out to investigate, he waited till daybreak, when he found two muddy paw-marks on the sill and enormous footprints all over the grass. In this case the intruder proved to be an escaped wallaby *en route* from East Grinstead to Horsham where it was caught, but not before nearly causing a nasty accident by leaping right over a moving car on the main road.

Extension

Despite the transfer in 1970 of Scottish teachers' pensions to the Scottish Education Department, the general tendency since dispersal has been for other departments to recognise and enhance the cost effectiveness of the PGO's pension-paying system by transferring to it additional work of a similar nature. In the space of only six years the PGO took over the issue and payment of private car allowances, car maintenance allowances, pensions to retired employees of the Customs and Excise, Inland Revenue, Queen's and Lord Treasurer's Remembrancer and Forestry Commission, and the pensions of the other ranks of the air force and navy — over 70,000 new pension accounts in all. Although the growth in staff numbers had slowed since the creation of the SSU, the volume of pensions increased from 400,000 at the end of 1962 to 700,000 in December 1974. There were also increases in staff caused by both the growth in banking work (11 million payments in 1962; 18 million in 1974) and the need for larger systems and programming teams in preparation for replacement computers. The design of Sutherland House had allowed for 'normal' growth, yet within three years of the end of dispersal consideration had to be given to providing an additional 36,000 square feet of office space.

This requirement coincided with the need for a 9,000 square feet extension to the computer hall, so that the new computers planned for 1976 could be set up and tested before taking over live work from their predecessors. Tenders were invited in 1974 for the erection of a five-storey, L-shaped extension, designed by architects of the Property Services Agency, Department of the Environment. The contract was awarded to Miller Buckley Construction Ltd, and work began in April 1975 on a site formerly occupied by walled flower beds and a paved area with seats. Unlike the building of the original office the eastern extension arose in full view of the PGO staff, for whom the hoisting and fixing of massive girders, the adept balancing acts of the workmen and the suspension of concrete facing panels provided a fascinating diversion from their normal duties.

The new wing incorporated on the ground floor an air conditioning plant and data preparation room to accommodate enlarged key-to-disc systems, while the upper floors were linked to the original building by a novel feature, born of necessity. Because building specifications had been metricated since the design of the original office the modular sections of the new wing would not abut neatly to those of the old, and the architect's remedy was to link the two by a glass-sided, unheated bridge in which each floor sloped at a slightly different angle. Rooms in the extension were generally darker because the windows were smaller, but it was carpeted throughout (an innovation later extended to the rest of the office) and generally those who moved into it in October 1976 felt honoured to be the

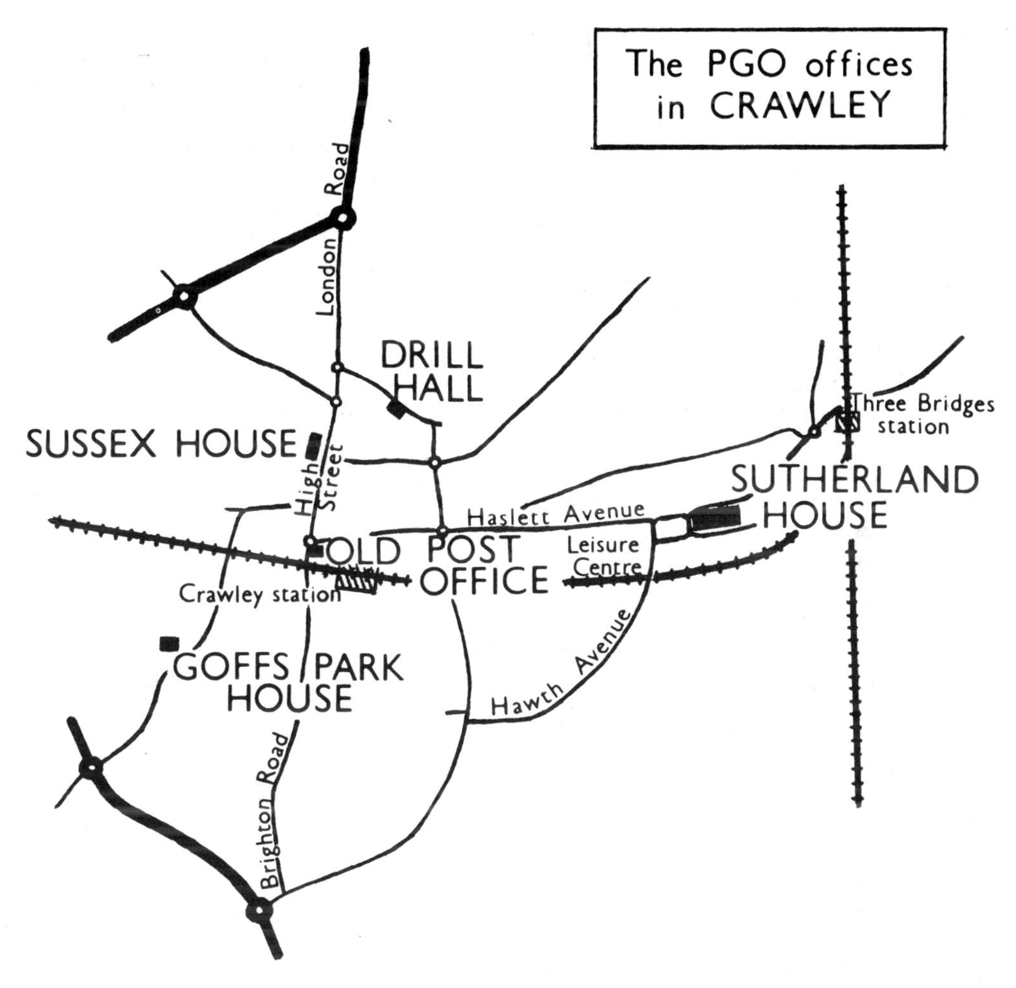

first to sample its newness. Initially the PGO could not fill all of the extra space because this, too, allowed for future growth, and the fourth floor was let to the Health and Safety Executive until 1979. In 1980 the water-cooled air-conditioning plant which had created vibration, noise and condensation was replaced by air-cooled chillers on the roof; during the removal of the obsolete machinery the Office suffered its only serious incident at Crawley when a workman's blowlamp started a fire which sent up clouds of black smoke before being extinguished by the fire brigade.

The years 1977-9 were eventful. The PGO's new APEX computer system was implemented, in order to provide the Treasury speedily with up to date information on spending by government departments; the new Administration vote was set up, with the Assistant Paymaster General as Accounting Officer — the first time the Office had been accountable for its own expenditure since 1890, although the Treasury retained responsibility for both the department's banking policy and the appointment of the Assistant Paymaster General and his deputies; and a new State pensions scheme caused unprecedented problems in the pension divisions. Subsequent years have witnessed numerous reviews of personnel policy, in matters such as race relations, sexual discrimination and harassment, equal opportunities, work sharing and the employment of disabled people. Examinations of the necessity and cost of the Office's tasks have become a regular feature, and the department has an obligation to carry out an Efficiency Scrutiny every other year. The first of these led to the closure in 1980 of the Eagle House branch office, when its work was taken over by the Bank of England, while the second resulted in a reduction in the requirement for periodic attested declarations from pensioners. Similar scrutinies in the awarding departments produced recommendations for the PGO to take on the payment of the army's other ranks pensioners, and for teachers' pension awards to be transmitted by magnetic tape.

In 1983 the Paymaster General, Cecil Parkinson, commissioned Messrs Coopers and Lybrand Associates to examine the possibility of privatising the issue and payment of the public service pensions handled by the PGO. Its cleaning, gardening and night security services were already put out to contract. It came as no surprise to an Office proud of its tradition of cost-effective service to learn the consultants main conclusion: 'the benefits of further improvements to pension provision within a civil service framework are likely to outweigh any benefits which might result from privatisation'. It was a conclusion which was warmly welcomed by Mr Parkinson himself, who was already convinced of the PGO's efficiency. Since then, the department has continued to aim for ever greater efficiency and technological advance, to enhance the service it gives already to its pensioner and government customers.

The staff numbers, grades and pay scales at 1 April 1985 were as follows:

1	*Assistant Paymaster General (grade 5)*	*£20964 - £25533*
2	*senior principals (grade 6)*	*£17000 - £22926*
6	*principals*	*£13508 - £18363*
20	*senior executive officers (SEO)*	*£10980 - £13801*
62½	*higher executive officers (HEO)*	*£8896 - £11265*
151½	*executive officers (EO)*	*£4953 - £8917*
384½	*clerical officers (CO)*	*£3149 - £6293*
116	*clerical assistants (CA)*	*£2898 - £5054*
12½	*senior data processors (SDP)*	*£5705 - £6907*
38	*data processors (DP)*	*£4485 - £5688*
2	*personal secretaries*	*£5322 - £6607*
1	*superintendent of typists*	*£6764 - £7493*
6½	*typists*	*£3951 - £5054*
2	*photoprinters*	*£4772 - £5574*
3	*security officers*	*£4622 - £5671*
1	*office keeper*	*£6780 - £7895*
3	*senior messengers*	*£5219 - £5510*
11½	*messengers*	*£4534 - £5081*
4	*porter/messengers*	*£4534 - £5081*
1	*senior paperkeeper*	*£5422 - £6217*
5	*paperkeepers*	*£5219 - £5510*
3	*telephonists*	*£2904 - £5185*
837		

10. BANKING : *a service to Government*

Balances

The concept of the PGO as paying agent and banker for all government spending departments has not changed since 1848, when the Office became responsible for paying civil as well as the armed services. It is founded on three main principles:

1. payments are best made in a different place from where they are certified, in the interests of security;

2. a single pay office is bound to be more economical and efficient than several detached offices; and

3. a unified pay office minimises the overall bank balance and therefore government borrowing.

Although the PGO now administers within its own books about 400 accounts for government departments and receives payment authorities from 1,000 separate issuing points in respect of more than 30 million payments a year, it maintains only four accounts at the Bank of England. Briefly, the system works as follows. Each day the Office requisitions from the nation's Consolidated Fund sufficient money to meet the expected payments for the day. This goes into the EXCHEQUER SUPPLY ACCOUNT. The other receipt account is the CASH ACCOUNT, to which are credited sums which other government departments obtain — for example, licence fees, admission charges and fines paid into court. From these two accounts are transferred funds to enable the two paying accounts to meet their daily commitments. The BILL ACCOUNT makes payments for Bills of Exchange and the DRAWING ACCOUNT all other payments, by payable order and pension voucher presented through the clearing banks, or by write-off to non-PGO accounts at the Bank of England, such as those of the Post Office, Customs and Excise and National Giro. Payments due from one customer department to another are made by internal transfer within the PGO's books without the need to trouble the Bank.

When the Office was set up in 1836 it opened an Exchequer Supply, Cash and two Drawing accounts, one each for effective and non-effective (pension) services. Two years later, on the recommendation of Sir Henry Parnell, the Drawing accounts were amalgamated and the Bill account opened. There have been no other changes in the PGO's bank accounts in 147 years. Only the Treasury may authorise the release of money from the Consolidated Fund, and then only with the approval of the National Audit Office. However, within its own four bank accounts the PGO has the sole discretion. In the 19th century the Assistant Paymaster General (or his deputy) had to sign all requisitions from the Consolidated Fund and all write-offs to feed the paying accounts. Today he delegates these duties to two separate panels of signatories.

To achieve the long-standing aim of keeping the overall bank balances to a minimum, throughout most of each month the PGO makes payments for all services from the general balance at its disposal, regardless of the amounts drawn for individual departmental accounts. In this way the need to draw unnecessarily on the Consolidated Fund is avoided. Towards the end of each month drawings are adjusted so that departmental accounts stand in credit, but by that time the government has reaped substantial benefits by investing otherwise idle money. The Exchequer Supply account receives only sufficient to feed the Drawing account, so it has a nil balance at the end of each day. The Bill account, which is funded from the Cash Account, holds only enough to meet its known expenses. The Cash account maintains a balance which just covers the Bank's cost in handling the PGO and Treasury banking requirements and (since 1980) in processing the daily lodgment of orders and vouchers. Any excess on the Cash account is added daily to that of the Drawing account, and the surplus (above £1) on this is lent at the end of each day to the National Loans Fund, as a 'Ways and Means Advance' for reinvestment.

Within the PGO books detailed accounts are kept for each departmental vote so that shortly after the end of each month statements of receipts and payments may be issued. Until 1866 these were all sent direct to the Audit Office, but now they go to the customer departments, which render their own returns. The PGO was one of the government's pioneer users of double-entry book-keeping. It was introduced from the beginning, in 1836, and was so successful that in 1840 Parnell not only persuaded the Treasury to implement it in the War Office, but also lent a PGO man to steer it through. In 1871 the Office loaned a further accountant to assist the Customs and Excise in the same task.

Payment

Since the creation of the Office its staple diet has been the payment of salaries, wages and pensions, although amounts which are often much larger are involved in defence services, building works and farming subsidies. Old correspondence registers recall many interesting transactions of the past, such as the payment in 1859 of £38.16.3d 'for repair to the French Admiral's barge, in consequence of its having been smashed by the British Barque, Queen of Newfoundland'. Over the years the amounts handled have increased considerably, from £11 million in 1837 to £258,485 million in 1985. The number of payments rose from 180,000 in 1859/60 (the earliest year for which precise figures exist) to 36 million in 1983/4. Methods also have changed, but the one constant factor has been the PGO's insistence on paying nothing unless satisfied that it has been properly authorised.

In the earliest days of the PGO, the most common method of payment was the receipt, or voucher. For effective services, this was a form which the authorising department handed to the payee at the same time as it sent the PGO a schedule of authorised payments. The claimant had to complete and sign the receipt and take it to the PGO at either Whitehall or Dublin Castle, where it was first examined to see that it had been correctly completed, and then compared with the schedule to ensure that it was properly payable. Next, the examiner assessed income tax, made the deduction, signed the form and handed it back to the claimant who then took it to the pay room. There it was scrutinised again (to ensure that an examiner had passed it for payment), and finally the payee received either a cheque drawn on the Bank of England or Ireland, or cash if the amount was below a certain limit (£10 in 1838; £100 in 1898). In the case of non-effective payments, departments sent to the PGO lists of the persons authorised to receive pensions, and the Office issued the necessary voucher as and when payment fell due, on personal application by the pensioner. At each stage, a record had to be kept of the action taken, to prevent double payment on the same voucher, and such was the complexity of the whole process that it is no wonder there was congestion in the pay rooms at the end of each quarter, when salaries and pensions were due.

The practice of having payees call personally at the Office was not without its hazards. In 1851 the Treasury asked the PGO to be prepared to pay accumulated earnings to 'a large number of liberated convicts' about to be released from captivity in Bermuda. William Anderson resisted this on the grounds that it was not 'the most convenient course'. Instead, he urged that the convicts be paid in Bermuda before their discharge, although he did concede to pay any who were already on their way. In 1871 the seamen's allotments (to their dependants) had to be dispensed from a nearby workhouse room, as a precautionary measure during an epidemic of smallpox in the navy.

Alternative means of payment existed for people who could not get to London or Dublin, but it was not until the 20th century that the Office would entrust payable documents to the postal service. The PGO therefore used local 'paying officers' to act as its agents. Most of these were officials of other government departments, but the PGO's own staff at Hanover and the dockyards operated in a similar way. Many paying officers (including the ports staff) required 'imprest' advances in the form of bills of exchange or shipments of cash before they dispensed money on the PGO's behalf. For the armed services the paying officers were private firms such as Cox and Co, who called themselves 'army agents'. The army also had its own cashiers at the Royal Gunpowder Factory, and the navy stationed cashiers at the dockyards after closure of the PGO offices in 1856. For civil payments in the United Kingdom the Office frequently used Collectors of Customs and Excise and Inland Revenue; in foreign countries payments were made through British Consuls; and in the Colonies the imprest was held by 'Treasury Chest' officers at stations as widely spread as Gibraltar, Cape Town, Colombo and Halifax, Nova Scotia. The overseas and PGO paying officers each held a padlocked chest containing reserves of cash sufficient to meet expenditure for two months. Not surprisingly, great security surrounded the shipments of coin: when ships loaded with thousands of gold sovereigns and silver pieces were despatched it was essential for a PGO employee to attend the loading and for the imprest officer to count them on arrival. In 1854 the Colonial Treasury Chests were being funded additionally from customs duties and the proceeds from the sale of captured slave trade vessels. The voucher system was used for payments by imprest officers, and all paid vouchers eventually found their way back to the PGO in Whitehall. After all action had been completed they were sent to the authorising departments, except for civil superannuation vouchers, which went to the Audit office.

The Office needed to hold large sums of cash, to pay individuals and to make advances of imprest. Between 1836 and 1841 the cash payments at Whitehall were made by two Bank of England cashiers, whose services cost the department £700 a year. In 1841, when the Office was allowed to select its own cashier, it chose Thomas Morris, a principal clerk. The lucky man was granted an allowance of £100 a year, but had to supply a bond of £2,000 and two sureties of £1,000 each. Sufficient cash to meet the day's requirements was collected daily

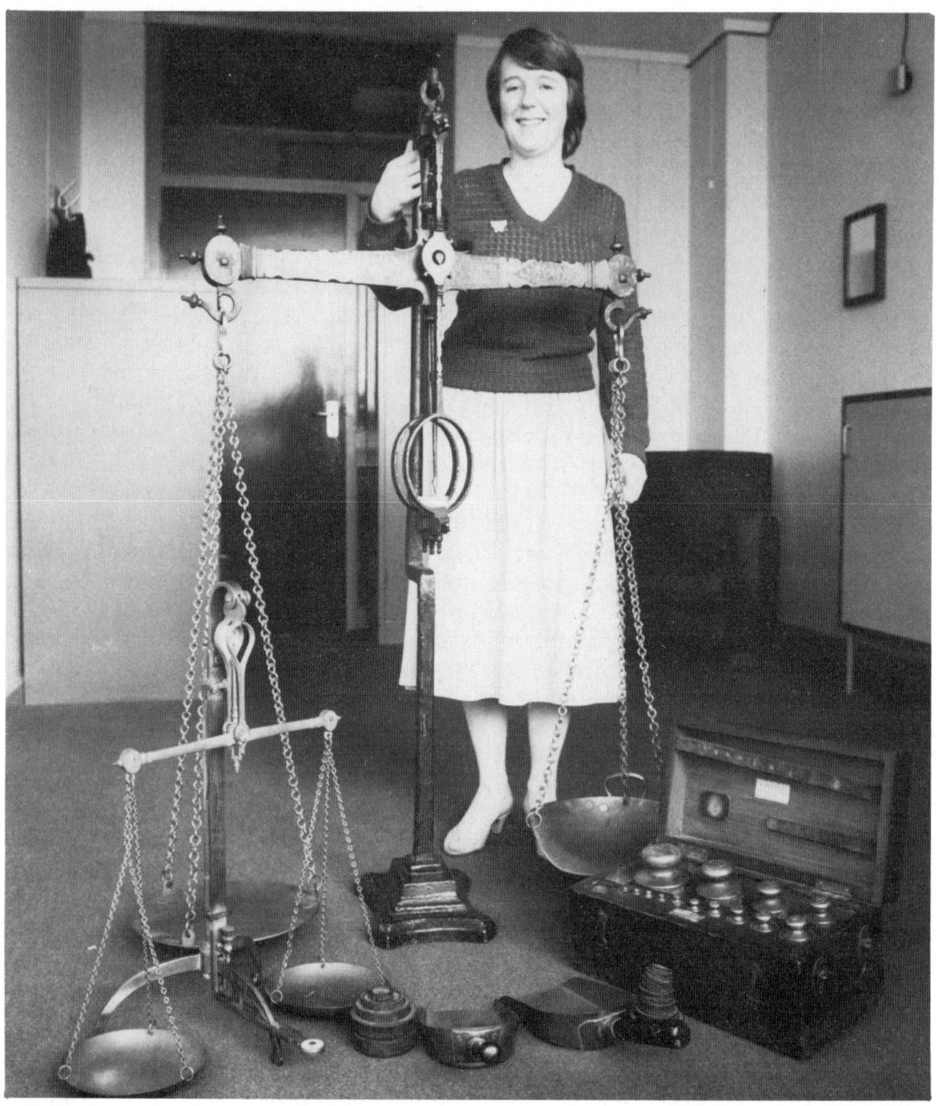

CASH WEIGHING APPARATUS formerly used in the PGO: the largest balances bear the date 1909.
Photo: Ken Bridle, 1985.

from the Bank of England and brought back to the Office by the cashier (or 'paymaster') in a taxi-cab. Once in 1862 there was panic when the paymaster, Alfred Earnshaw, failed to appear at the Office with the cash until 12 noon. He had taken home the cheque necessary to draw it from the Bank, only to be delayed next morning by a railway accident which left him stranded beyond Dartford. The Assistant Paymaster General was not amused. 'As accidents are not of infrequent occurrence on railways', he proclaimed in ponderous Victorian prose, 'the Paymaster should on these occasions either sleep in Town or adopt some other course, to obviate the possibility of the whole Office being thrown into a state of confusion in consequence of his detention through any irregularity which may occur on the Railway'.

In 1867 the Treasury decided that civil service salaries should be paid monthly rather than quarterly; two years later civil service pensions followed suit. This was greeted with foreboding at the PGO, which feared that the peak of work suffered by examiners and pay clerks would be experienced 12 times a year instead of four. As payment was still confined to the last day of each month, the Office tried to get the load spread more evenly by asking some departments to send their salary lists in advance, already receipted by the payees. This enabled the PGO to deliver the payments on pay-day, either in the form of payable orders to be handed out by the departments' own officials, or in cash, dispensed by two PGO cashiers. In 1879 the Treasury agreed that cash payments could be made by the customer departments, under imprest arrangements. This, they said, would 'effect a very appreciable reduction of labour at the Pay Office'. By the end of the century most large departments were paying their own salaries, but as late as 1917 the PGO was writing and assessing tax on more than 10,000 orders a year for the rest. In that year, the Office finally discontinued this service as part of its drive to make the best of its resources in the war.

The PGO still needed to hold cash for pensioners, and customer departments requiring coin imprest. Although in 1919 departments were authorised to open imprest accounts at local banks, many continued to use the facilities at the PGO's Whitehall office. Occasionally there was no need to collect cash from the Bank because some departments had deposited sufficient in respect of passport fees, Stationery Office sales, and conscience money, received by the Treasury from repentant tax-dodgers. However, on most days between the wars PGO staff collected cash in a bullion van each morning and checked it on arrival at the Office by weighing it on heavy, brass scales, nearly five feet high. An attempted robbery of government money and an outbreak of smash-and-grab raids in 1932 led to a round-table conference between the PGO, Treasury, Office of Works and Metropolitan Police. It emerged that two Bank porters and a private detective were constantly present at each loading, the drivers were 'subject to elaborate precautions', the messengers were 'reliable men', and back at the PGO up to nine men were on hand to supervise the unloading. The only improvement found necessary was to deliver the cash not at the front door in Whitehall but through an entrance off the Horse Guards yard, for which the King's Life Guard would need to unlock the stables gate. After that, security seems to have lapsed, because in the late 1930s Admiralty staff were openly collecting sums of up to £200,000 in cash from the PGO on a trolley which they wheeled along the street into their premises next door.

Even when the Office was in Russell Square cash was being collected from the Bank, in a van manned by a driver, the PGO cashier and two ageing messengers. Incredibly, there was never any incident to threaten its security, although on one occasion the police were alerted when someone dropped a cash bag on the alarm button. In the 1950s the Office was still paying cash to over 50 government departments, at a cost to the PGO alone of over £5,000 a year, and with increasing risk to its staff. It was the radical Mr Vetch who managed to end the practice. In 1957 he persuaded the Treasury to instruct all departments (some of which were travelling from as far afield as Southwark and Kensington) to draw their cash at a local bank, and not from the PGO. The daily van trip to the Bank of England ceased, and the Office began to collect cash for its own purposes (salaries, petty expenses and some pensions) from the branch of Barclay's which was built conveniently into the corner of Russell Square House. At the same time, Mr Vetch stopped the payment of cash for all new pensions and the salaries of EOs and higher ranks in the PGO. When the Office began to leave London in 1964 only petty expenses and the wages of weekly-paid staff were being paid in cash. In Crawley, a small supply was collected weekly from a branch bank in Three Bridges, until in 1981 the payment of all wages in cash came to an end.

The payable orders which departments began to use in the 19th century ceased to require a signature as a receipt in 1964. However, they still needed to be checked at the PGO against the schedules of issues, and pension vouchers had to be compared with the ledger sheets, so just after the end of each month when thousands of orders were presented by the banks, examination kept many staff at work well into the evening. The task of sorting and checking was speeded in 1918 when serial numbering and a uniform size of payable order were adopted, and in 1937 some of the urgency was removed by the decision to pay the bank claims 'at sight', without previous examination. Nevertheless, the matching of payments with issues remained a laborious clerical chore until it was computerised in 1970. Before mechanisation in 1957-61 the clerks examining pension vouchers had an additional check to carry out: the comparison of signatures with those on the original applications for payment. Even after mechanisation sample checks continued, but with the advent of direct payment to bank accounts (introduced as an experiment in 1964) the need for these has diminished. However, the PGO still honours its obligation to make only payments which have been properly authorised, by performing a check on the departmental authorising signatures which accompany every effective schedule and pension award.

No payments are now made through regimental agents or revenue Collectors, bills of exchange are a rarity, and overseas paying officers are used only for locally engaged staff whose pensions are awarded in foreign currency. There is a growing tendency for pensions to be paid by direct credit to the pensioner's bank account, through the Bankers' Automated Clearing Services (BACS), first used in 1979. Now, two thirds of all pensions issued by the PGO are paid in this way. The payable order method is still the simplest for effective payments which are isolated amounts to contractors, farmers and individual members of the public. However, many departments now issue some regular payments such as salaries and pensions through BACS, and this has accounted for a slight decline in the number of transactions handled by the PGO over the last two years. In 1984/5 the volume was reduced also by a strike at the Department of Health and Social Security which affected the issue of State pensions.

Claims

Another labour-intensive and time-critical task ever since the creation of the Office has been that of agreeing the banks' claims by adding all the amounts on payable orders and pension vouchers received in the daily lodgment. Despite being helped around the end of the Great War by the introduction of add-list machines, lodgment processing remained a significant daily chore until the arrival in 1969 of machines capable of reading a magnetically encoded line on each order and voucher. Bank agreement was not fully automated at the PGO until 1983.

The bank lodgment was the sole justification for the caller office set up in

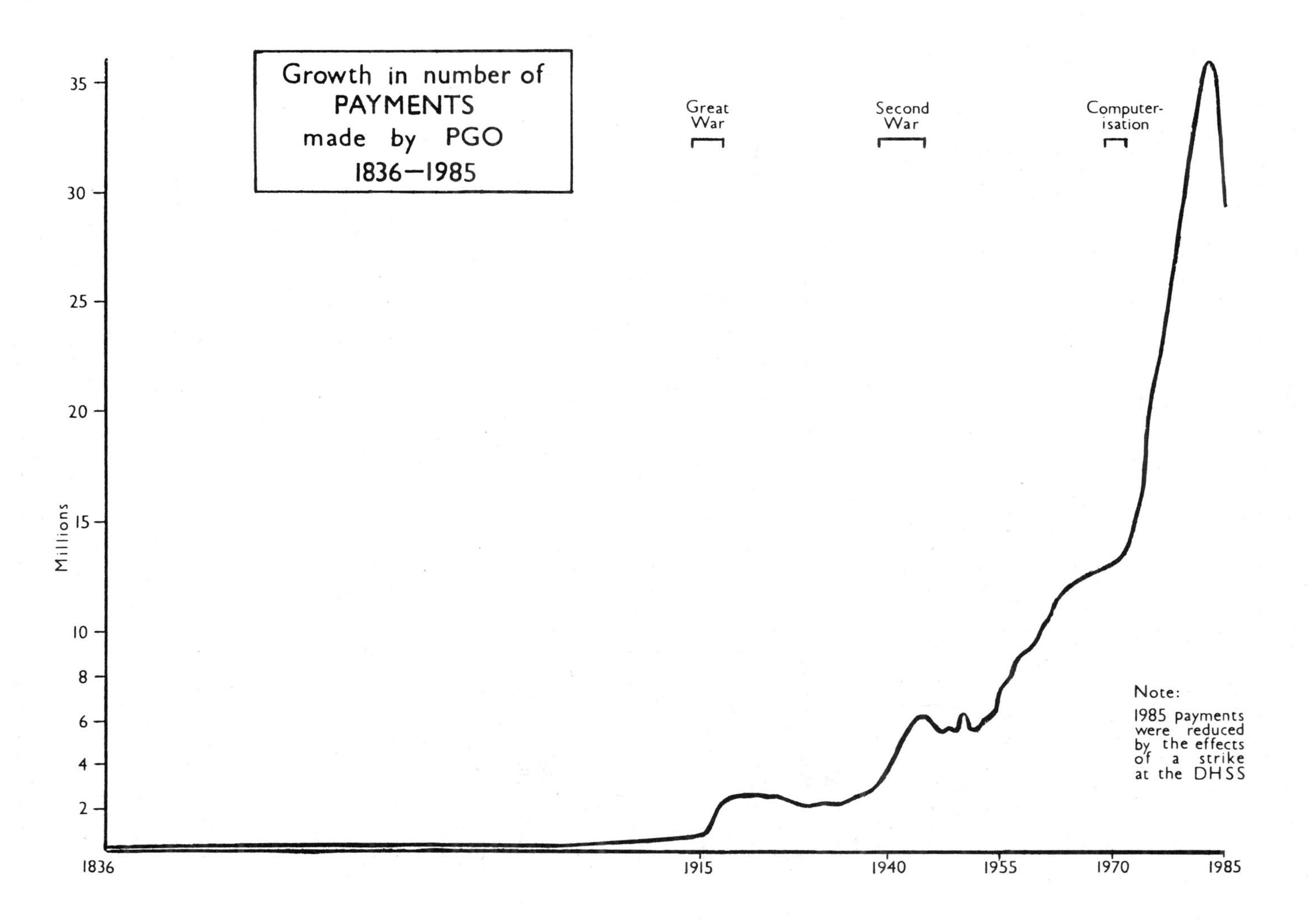
Growth in number of
PAYMENTS
made by PGO
1836–1985
Great
War
Second
War
Computer-
isation
35
30
25
20
15
10
8
6
4
2
Millions
Note:
1985 payments
were reduced
by the effects
of a strike
at the DHSS
1836
1915
1940
1955
1970
1985

EAGLE HOUSE, Cannon Street: branch office 1971-80.
Photo: Ken Bridle, 1984.

London when the rest of the department dispersed to Crawley. The location of the PGO in Whitehall, Somerset House and Russell Square had always been inconvenient for the clearing banks which called daily to present their claims, and no doubt they were delighted when in November 1971 their PGO contact point was moved to the City. It was staffed by only 2 EOs, 2 COs and a senior messenger, housed in one ground floor room of Eagle House, near Cannon Street station. Each morning the banks would deliver their consignment of payable orders and vouchers, and receive a clearing voucher which the Bank messenger presented at the Bank of England. Eagle House staff had to send the lodgment on to Crawley by the official van service, after first sorting and detailing the lump sums, which were still processed manually. They kept in touch with the rest of the Office and received instructions from the FD book-keeping section by telephone and by a new facsimile transmission link, MUFAX. The work continued even when delivery vans were halted at the picket line during a strike of computer operators in 1979. For the first few days Eagle House staff collected the lodgment from the Bank and pushed it through the streets of London on hand-trolleys; later on they sorted the vouchers at the Bank and sent the lodgment direct to Crawley from there.

Towards the end of 1979 the Bank of England offered to receive the daily lodgment, process it through the Bank's own computer and issue to the PGO a magnetic tape of the details necessary to agree the banks' claims and match items with the schedules. Following an Efficiency Scrutiny the Office agreed, and vacated Eagle House in August 1980. For the next three years the Bank merely replaced the caller office in acting as the central point for collecting the lodgment, but when the Bank's new computer system was implemented it began to supply the PGO with the promised tape in October 1983.

APEX

Associated with the Office's long-established banking service is a comparatively new addition to the PGO repertoire: APEX, a computer system for the Analysis of Public EXpenditure. Early in 1975 the Treasury unveiled a new plan for monitoring and controlling public expenditure; it bore the effervescent acronym 'FIS' (Financial Information System). Originally the idea was that each department would send to the Treasury both estimates of likely spending during a financial year and monthly returns of actual expenditure, split into precise categories. However, it was clear that much of the data on actual spending was already available at the PGO, on the schedules of payments sent in by authorising departments. With adaptation the PGO banking system could save other departments the trouble of sending separate returns to the Treasury, and it could aggregate and analyse the statistics in exactly the form which the Treasury required.

Assistant Paymaster General Freddie Clay was eager for the Office to work with the Treasury on the project. He therefore detached Ray Heavens from his post of ADP Systems and Programming Manager to assess the additional data which the PGO would need, and to find out whether the departments would have any difficulty in providing it. He travelled the length and breadth of the country to sell the PGO option to departments, and by the end of 1975 the government had been persuaded that it was far better than the original plan. Because the Office's systems staff were fully engaged already on enhancements to the existing pensions and banking systems, the PGO accepted the job on condition that the Treasury would arrange the return of its first banking analyst, Dennis Breed, from the Civil Service Department to which he had been transferred in 1970. He and a senior consultant from Coopers and Lybrand Associates began early in 1976 to design a new computer system to process the payment schedules and to handle additional input from the revenue departments, which did not use the PGO banking service. Despite some reservations about its connection with a trade union and a local cleaning firm, the title APEX was adopted.

The system was implemented in April 1977, only partially at first as some departments had not overcome all of their problems, but eventually APEX was able to provide monthly information of expenditure under 5,000 categories, on magnetic tapes sent to the Treasury. There the tapes are input to FIS and reports are produced to compare the amounts spent with the monthly 'profile' forecasts. In this way APEX has supplemented the vital service which the PGO banking system gives to government.

11. PENSIONS : *a personal service*

Schemes

Although the majority of transactions handled by the PGO have always been effective payments, it is in the administration of non-effective payments — the pensions — that most of the staff have been employed. Today more than 85 per cent of the clerical staff are to be found in the pension divisions. The reason is the on-going responsibility which the PGO has for superannuation awards. Before 1836 the pay offices of the navy and ordnance had required a separate authority for each instalment of pension, but the new-born PGO was to adopt the system used in the army pay office, where a pension award authorised continuing payment for as long as the pensioner was entitled — usually until death. Thus from the first day the Office's clerks had responsibility for dealing with correspondence throughout the lifetime of each pension, and for issuing payments which took account of the latest information on name, address, pension rate, tax and so on.

In its first 150 years the Office has issued and paid pensions to a wide variety of public servants under a varied range of schemes. The few thousand which it inherited in 1836 from the ARMED FORCES pay offices were themselves a hotch potch of retired pay, half pay, widows' pensions and disability pay which had been awarded at the discretion of the service departments with little regard for consistency. For commissioned officers there could be no regular superannuation system while they continued to buy and sell commissions — a practice which stopped only in 1871 — so from time to time they were placed on retired or half pay lists simply to improve the promotion prospects of the younger men. Nor was there any systematic provision for either families or other ranks, although such pensions were awarded occasionally, and Chelsea and Greenwich Hospital out-pensions were granted for some soldiers and seamen who had become 'maimed or worn out' in the service of their country. The present day non-contributory forces pensions scheme, which originated in Acts of 1865 (navy), 1884 (army) and 1917 (air force), provides for retired pay to regular commissioned officers, pensions to other ranks and, since 1973, family pensions to their widows and children. Half pay has not been awarded since 1980.

Quite apart from this scheme there is provision for compensation to servicemen (including non-regulars) and their families in the event of death or disability on active service. Such payments have been made since at least the 18th century, and have reflected the tragedy of conflicts such as the Crimea and Boer wars, the two world wars and the more recent troubles in Korea, the Falklands and Northern Ireland. Disability pay is often complicated by the range of special allowances granted for age, invalidity, unemployability, medical treatment, clothing and other factors.

Strangely enough, despite its proven record of economy and efficiency, the PGO does not pay all forces pensions. Some of the schemes came into being

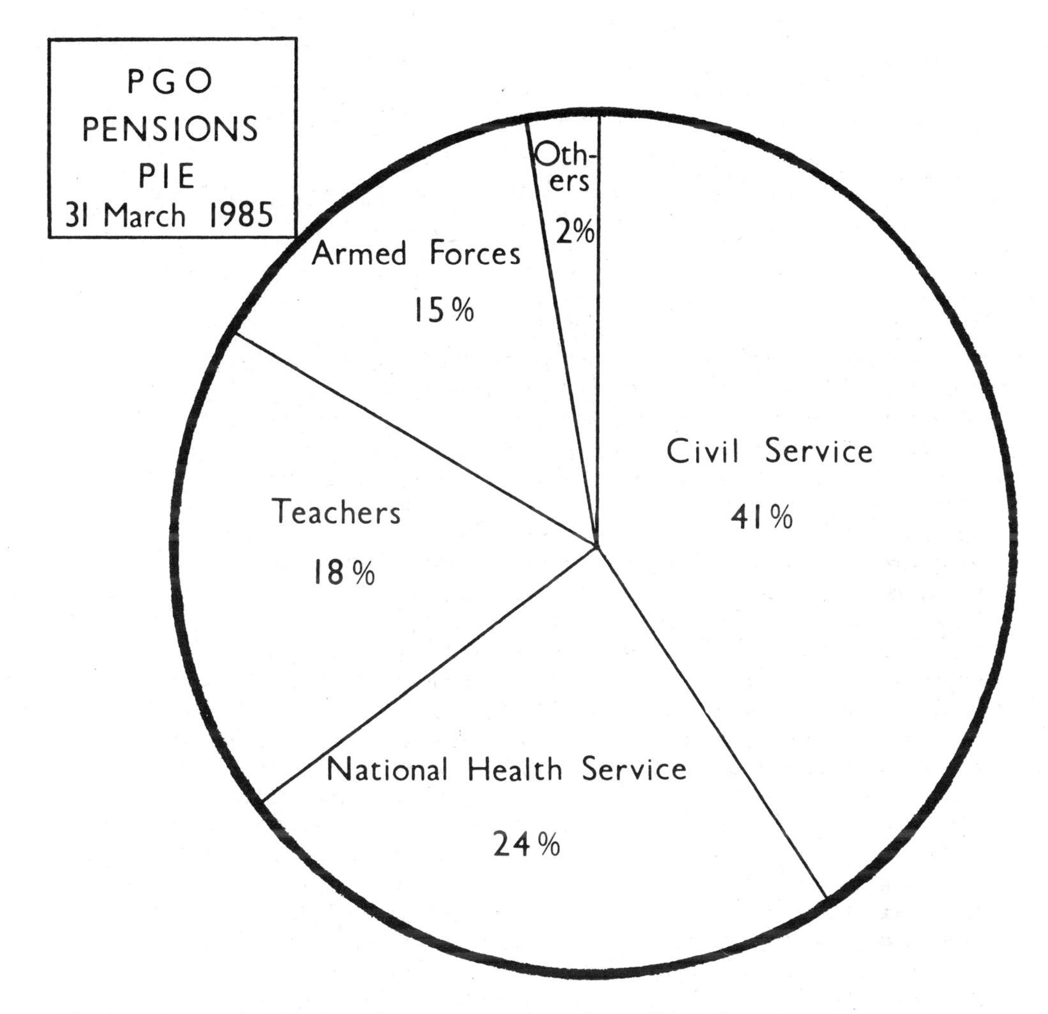

during that period in the 19th century when the Office's future was uncertain, so the pensions were issued by service paymasters. It was not until the 1970s that the PGO took over payment of most other ranks pensions, and even now (1985) the Ministry of Defence pays all of the army other ranks and those of the navy and air force who ask for weekly payment. Among the more unusual pensions and annuities now paid by the Office are those due to holders of the Victoria Cross and George Cross, Army nurses and school-mistresses (since 1909) and beneficiaries of the Drouly and Travers Estate charities, which originated in the 19th century. For 10 years from 1836 the PGO paid Greenwich Hospital out-pensions from its office at Tower Hill, while some Chelsea out-pensions were paid in Hanover until that office closed in 1862. The only recorded payments direct to Chelsea Hospital were for in-pension charges and the cost of trusses for the pensioners in 1848.

With the second consolidation in 1848 the Office took on the payment of CIVIL SERVICE pensions. A scheme applicable to all established (male) civil servants had been enacted in 1810, replacing various departmental schemes which had developed since Customs set the pace in 1712. When taken over by the PGO, the pensions were governed by an Act of 1834, which provided for contributory, tax-free pensions payable at the age of 65 (or earlier in the case of ill health), up to a maximum of two thirds of retiring salary for those with 45 years' service. Civil servants in post before 1830 enjoyed a non-contributory scheme with even better benefits, including a pension equal to half salary after 20 years' service, and full salary equivalent if they survived in the job for 50 years.

In 1857 direct contributions were discontinued, and two years later pensions became payable at the age of 60. From 1909 they were calculated as one eightieth of retiring salary for each year of service (instead of one sixtieth, under the 1859 Act). While this meant that 40 years' service was rewarded by a pension of only half salary instead of two thirds, there was some recompense in the form of a lump sum payment, up to a maximum of 1½ times the retiring salary. The lump sum provisions were extended to women in 1935. Men serving in 1909 and women in 1935 were given the choice of retaining the benefits of the 1859 Act. The 1935 Act also made the first provision for surrender of part of a pension in return for an allowance to a spouse or dependant. In 1949 a contributory scheme began which gave pensions to widows, children and dependants after the employee's death. A long succession of Superannuation Acts ended with that of 1972, which sanctioned the administration of schemes without the need for further statutory authority: it was followed by a new 'Principal Civil Service Pension Scheme' which included many improvements, such as the increase in widow's entitlement from one third to one half of her husband's pension. 1972 was also the point when civil servants fulfilling certain basic conditions could expect a pension as of right, and not at the Treasury's discretion.

Since 1848 the PGO has paid all civil service pensions except those of the revenue departments which it eventually took on in 1972-4. They embrace the whole range of retired civil servants, including ambassadors, permanent secretaries, prison officers (who receive pension from the age of 55), clerks, typists and labourers in overseas dockyards. The Civil Superannuation vote, for which the Assistant Paymaster General is accountable to parliament, now includes the RIC pensions transferred to the PGO in 1922, certain judicial pensions and some payments due to former employees of bodies which the government has nationalised or wound up, like the Friendly Societies, and Wheat, Raw Cotton and Development Commissions. It has also paid specially awarded pensions to former lock-keepers of the Caledonian Canal and the relatives of Captain Scott's ill-fated last expedition to the Antarctic. In 1978 retired staff of the Forestry Commission joined the ranks of pensioners paid by the PGO.

The development of a superannuation scheme for TEACHERS was much slower than that for civil servants, because their pay and conditions were in the hands of scores of local authorities which did not always see eye to eye. Awards of teachers' pensions began to be made in 1846, but the benefits were payable only in the event of incapacity, could be withdrawn if the teacher had 'sufficient means of livelihood from other sources' and, between 1851 and 1884 were restricted at any one time to only 270 pensions worth a total of £6,500 a year. An Act of 1898 set up a scheme for elementary school teachers which allowed them to contribute to a 'deferred annuity', payable at the age of 65, or at the end of their service if later. In 1918 contributions were abolished, only to be resumed four years later and supplemented from 1926 by contributions from the local education authorities. The 1918 Act lowered the qualifying age to 60, introduced lump sum payments and generally brought teachers' pensions into line with those in the civil service scheme; unlike civil superannuation, however, the teachers' scheme was directly contributory and not confined to the male sex. From 1937 retiring teachers were allowed to surrender part of their pension to secure an allowance to a spouse or dependant, but it was not until 1966 that a contributory scheme for family benefits was introduced.

The PGO has paid pensions to teachers formerly employed in England and Wales, continuously since 1899, apart from a seven year spell from 1919 when they were issued from the Board of Education. Scottish teachers remained with the PGO from 1899 until 1970, when they were transferred to the Scottish Education Department at that office's request. The Office also paid retired teachers from Jersey, Guernsey and the Isle of Man until 1979, when these pensions were taken over by the island authorities. Since 1975 it has also administered compensation payments to teaching and other staff who have been made redundant by the closure of Colleges of Education and Direct Grant schools. The PGO ceased issuing lump sum payments to all teachers in 1984, when that task was transferred to the Department of Education and Science at Darlington.

Newest and fastest growing of the major pension schemes for which the PGO makes payments is that of the NATIONAL HEALTH SERVICE (NHS), which came into operation in 1948. Because it was a late starter, the NHS scheme started with most of the features which it had taken the older schemes years to achieve. It is financed by contributions from the participants and central government funds, and provides for pension and lump sum payments from the age of 60, or 55 in the case of mental health officers and female nurses or midwives. Pensions are equivalent to one eightieth of retiring salary for every year of service, and lump sums are three times the annual rate of pension. The only major changes since 1948 have been the provision of children's allowances in 1966, the increase in widows' pensions to one half of their husbands' in 1974, and provision in 1981 for compensation for premature retirement caused by redundancy or inefficiency. The NHS scheme embraces a wide range of health service employees including hospital consultants, doctors and dentists, all levels of nursing and midwifery staff, professional specialists such as pharmacists, physiotherapists and radiographers, ancillary staff including cooks, gardeners and porters, and administrative and clerical staff. All have had their pensions and lump sums issued by the PGO since the scheme began.

In the 1970s the Office began to make two new classes of payment on behalf of the Department of Health and Social Security (DHSS). CAR MAINTENANCE ALLOWANCES, payable to the users of disabled persons' cars supplied by the DHSS, are assessed according to the age of the vehicle and whether or not the user is entitled to an allowance for garaging. PRIVATE CAR ALLOWANCES are paid to severely disabled people who have their own car. Should a recipient of either allowance become permanently unable to walk because of physical disablement, the allowance is replaced by a Mobility Allowance, paid by the DHSS. For war pensioners a new, non-taxable Mobility Supplement supplanted private car allowances in 1983 and is progressively replacing car maintenance allowances as the cars reach the end of their useful lives. Its intention is to extend the help to all war pensioners who have difficulty in walking.

During the 19th century the number of pensions grew slowly and steadily as

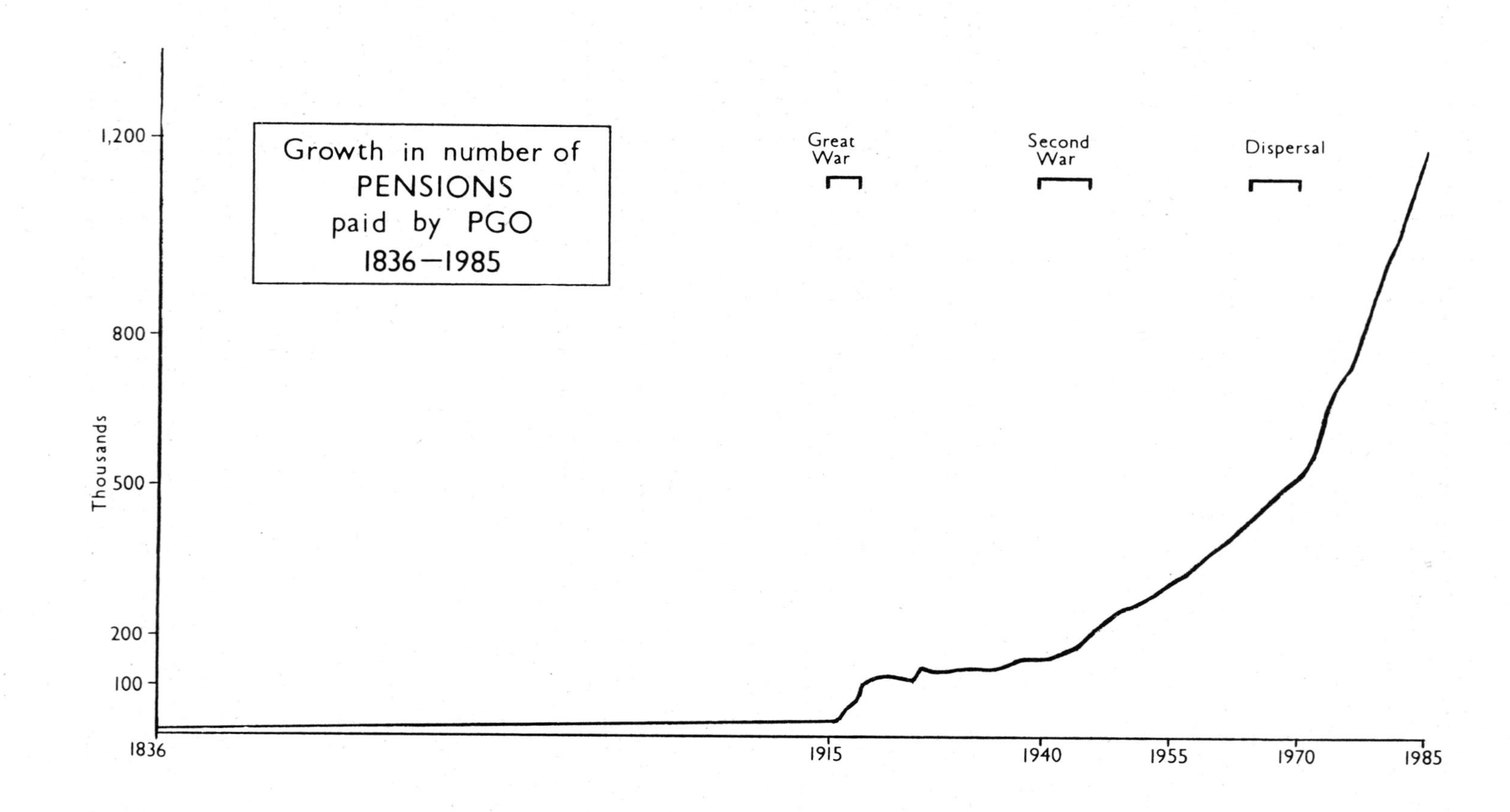
Growth in number of
PENSIONS
paid by PGO
1836—1985
Great War
Second War
Dispersal
1,200
800
500
200
100
Thousands
1836
1915
1940
1955
1970
1985

more public servants became eligible for superannuation under the new schemes. Even so, there were less than 30,000 at the turn of the century. The Great War was responsible for a four-fold increase by 1922, and four years later a further boost came with the return of teachers' pensions. In the inter-war years the growth in civil service and teachers numbers was almost offset by the deaths of war pensioners, but the Second World War increased the pension payroll to more than 200,000.

The addition of NHS, Customs, Inland Revenue and other pensions since 1948 has combined with an accelerating 'natural' growth rate due to the increasing size of the public services, the introduction of family pensions and, most recently, the incidence of premature retirements as the public services began to shrink once more. In 1963 the total reached 400,000, in 1978 it passed 800,000, and by the end of March 1985 it stood at 1,174,959. The growth rate is currently between 3 and 4 per cent a year.

Entitlement

One aspect of pension payment which has altered radically in the last 150 years is the extent to which a person claiming a pension must prove entitlement. Until 1835 claimants had to swear before a Commissioner of Oaths before their pension could be paid, but this was then relaxed in favour of a statutory declaration which had to be signed in the presence of a qualified attestor at the time of each payment. The requirement was so strictly adhered to that in 1861 the Office refused to accept declarations signed before the payment date because this fell on a Sunday. Qualification to attest was originally restricted to a very select band of highly trustworthy gentlemen, and as late as 1898 only people such as Justices of the Peace, Ministers of Religion, revenue and armed service paying officers and the PGO examining staff were on the list of those qualified. Over a period of many years the field of attestors has been broadened until today it comprises almost all of the adult population except for spouses. The frequency also has been relaxed, to quarterly in 1869, half-yearly in 1923, annually in 1933, three-yearly in 1969 and five-yearly ten years later. Following the Efficiency Scrutiny of 1982 declarations are now required even less frequently once a pension has begun, but pensioners are reminded from time to time of the conditions governing their entitlement.

Until 1957 the declaration of entitlement was an integral part of the pension voucher due for payment on the same date, but when mechanisation demanded standardisation in size, vouchers and declarations began to be issued separately. Mechanisation also accelerated progress towards uniform wording: because of the various requirements of each pension scheme in 1927 there were 300 different types of declaration form, but by 1975 these had been reduced to five.

The purpose of declarations was not just to ensure that the payee was the person named in the pension award. They called also for a statement that the pensioner fulfilled the requirements of the scheme, relating to re-employment, remarriage and even, in the Victorian era, good conduct. In 1904 attestors to teachers' declarations were still being asked to certify that the teacher's character was beyond reproach. There have been relaxations in the re-employment provisions over the years. For example, before the 1970s some of the PGO's pensions might be affected by employment in any part of the public service if the earnings were high enough, but now they are unaffected unless the re-employment is in the service from which the pension was earned. Also, abatements once had to be recalculated each time a re-employed pensioner received a pay rise, but this is no longer the case. Among the complications which still exist in re-employment work are the irregular earnings of pensioners such as doctors, dentists and supply teachers.

Recipients of widows' pensions have always been required to declare their marital status. This is because in most schemes paid by the PGO a widow's pension ceases on remarriage, except (since 1979) for the included portion representing the 'guaranteed minimum pension' (GMP) under the State pension scheme. In the 19th century much harsher conditions were attached to the award of pensions to armed services widows. As late as 1898 it was made clear that

> *they are granted as rewards for good and faithful service rendered by deceased Officers, . . . the Pensions are liable to be discontinued altogether, in the case of any misconduct rendering the individuals receiving them unworthy of the Public Bounty.*

Apart from misbehaviour a widow's pension could be stopped also if her private income exceeded amounts listed in a confidential scale, so the PGO examiners at that time were party to an unpopular means test each time a declaration was made. Despite all this the army department showed incredible leniency in the case of one widow who in 1853 was found to have been re-married to a known smuggler for the past 20 years. Approached by the PGO for instructions, the Secretary at War saw 'no ground for suspending the issue of the Pension', and the Paymaster General was quick to draw the Treasury's attention to a marked difference in treatment between the War Office and the Admiralty. Fraud and personation were particularly rife in the 19th century, especially in cases of payment to a third party when the pensioner became incapacitated. In 1849 things had become so bad that the Office employed a Metropolitan Police detective to pursue enquiries on its behalf. Within four years detective Thornton had brought to a conclusion more than 100 cases, including one conviction, and the Paymaster General pressed the Treasury to make a gratuity for his services.

Increases

Reliance upon the zeal of the examiners of old was such that until the 1920s pensioners who were not paid in cash were issued with a supply of blank vouchers on which they entered their name, address, payment date and even the amount which they were claiming. In 1923, however, following one of the few internal frauds discovered in the PGO, vouchers began to be serially numbered, and the dates and amounts entered and checked before issue. In any event it was becoming difficult for pensioners to state their pension amounts because in 1920 occurred the first Pensions (Increase) Act, to compensate for the rise in the cost of living since the Great War and to relieve the hardship of those who had been on fixed pensions for some time. Subsequent Acts in 1924, 1944, 1947 and 1952 gave flat rate or percentage increases which were subject to income and pension limits and varied with the date of commencement, size of pension and the pensioner's marital status. In 1956 the limitations of income and status were lifted, and although some of the larger pensions received increases for the first time, the concept of a maximum increase remained until the 1959 Act. This was the first of many simpler Acts which now recurred every three or four years to reflect the increasing rate of inflation. The pattern became established of percentage increases payable in most cases from the age of 60, the precise rate depending on the date the pension began. The 1962 Act, however, was complicated by an age 70 flat-rate addition which had to be apportioned if a payee was receiving more than one public service pension.

Income for the Pensions (Increase) Acts was not calculated in the same way as that for income tax, and the earlier means limits gave a lot of trouble to both pensioners and staff, especially in the recovery of overpayments. An especially troublesome feature was that a re-employed pensioner receiving an increase of salary could suffer not only a corresponding decrease of pension but also a reduction in pensions increase where this was a percentage of the rate in payment. Most of the anomalies were ironed out in the early 1970s. The 1971 Pensions (Increase) Act introduced a permanent basis of increases related to rises in the cost of living, and at the same time the rates of existing pensions were raised to compensate broadly for their decline in value since they were granted. Those with high salaries who had been on pension for many years benefited considerably: some pensions were almost doubled. In 1972 the qualifying age for increase was reduced to 55 years, and since then pensions increase has been awarded annually. From 1979 the rate and effective date have been in line with those of the State pension scheme, which in turn relates to the Cost of Living Index.

Needless to say, in the early days pensions increase generated much extra work for the PGO, which was responsible for obtaining certificates of income, making quite complex calculations without the aid of machines, and entering the new rates on ledger sheets. Each time a new Act was announced large numbers of students or other casual staff would be taken on until the exercise was completed. This remained the case until the Acts became simpler and the calculations were mechanised. Even then considerable overtime was needed in order to feed into the computer the basic details necessary to make the calculation, put the new rates into payment and update the ledger sheets. Not until the 1971 Act was pensions increase fully automated on the Office's new computer. From 1979, however, came an additional complication which is likely to cause increasing problems as time goes on. GMP to which pensioners are entitled under the State scheme is treated as part of the occupational pensions administered by the PGO, yet increases which it attracts are paid by the DHSS with State retirement pensions. This anomaly necessitates the identification of GMPs awarded to any PGO pensioner, apportionment of annual increases on the whole pension, and of course somewhat difficult correspondence with pensioners who cannot understand what is going on, or even what is GMP.

Service

Despite the constraints imposed by perpetual restrictions on public spending the PGO remains justly proud of the service it offers to pensioners. The Office has always been conscious of its duty to see that payments are made at the correct rate, to the correct payee, at the correct address, at the correct time. In the earliest days when civil servants were among the nation's elite the service offered usually ended there. Sometimes a rather superior and unfeeling attitude was taken with the more unfortunate pensioners who failed to understand the 'rules', and there was never any question of drawing attention to an unclaimed payment: a pension undrawn was forfeit. Fortunately a more helpful and sympathetic manner has prevailed since the last war.

Until comparatively recently the Office insisted on evidence that pensioners were alive on the payable date before making payment. In the case of those paid

PENSION SECTION 1931, in the converted fodder store (Room 1) at 36 Whitehall.
Photo: PGO archives.

by voucher such evidence is still required, in the form of the pensioner's signature on the voucher, on or after the due date. Before 1964 any pensioner who wanted a payment to go direct to his bank (for example, if he was overseas at the time) had to sign a 'life certificate' on the appropriate date, before the Office would release the voucher. An exception was made, however, in the case of incapacitated pensioners who could provide a power of attorney or (after 1939) sign an indemnity authorising alternative means of payment. Following the success of the experiment begun in 1964, payment to bank accounts was allowed on completion of an undertaking that any overpayment arising from the pensioner's death would be refunded. Since then, and particularly since the introduction in 1979 of direct credit transfer through BACS, successive campaigns have been mounted to persuade more pensioners to accept this more convenient method. As a result, about two thirds of the PGO's pensioners and nearly all new ones are now paid direct to their bank accounts, so avoiding the risk of postal delays and theft of vouchers. Even so, the Office still posts pension vouchers to all parts of Britain and 100 countries throughout the world.

Since the 1870s most pensioners have had a choice between quarterly and monthly payment, although teachers were not given the monthly option until 1957. When, in 1939, retiring civil servants were given the choice of weekly payment through a post office if they had been receiving weekly wages in employment, a new system had to be devised. Initially it was modelled on that adopted by the Post Office for its own pensioners, who received payment by pension orders, but in 1956 the PGO began to issue order books containing 13 weekly orders and counterfoils, similar to those in use for State pensions. By this time NHS weekly pensions were also being paid by the Office. When the Post Office became an independent corporation in 1969 it started to charge the PGO for its counter service and handling costs, and weekly paid pensions thus became more expensive to administer than their monthly and quarterly counterparts. However, the number has never exceeded 100,000, and it is now falling because fewer new pensioners are entitled or choose to be paid weekly.

The handling of correspondence is but one example of the service given to pensioners. Changes of address, notifications of re-employment or death, and queries about tax and 'broken period' calculations have been common features of the postbag for 150 years. More recently pensions increase, GMP and the restricted issue of advices where payment is made to banks have added to the mail, but fortunately reports of lost or delayed vouchers now are fewer since the introduction of the BACS alternative. Today most letters are answered by COs or EOs, using standard forms or typed replies, yet as recently as 1955 all of the less important typed letters were being signed by SEOs, and only seven years earlier the principal clerks were signing them all.

The present practice of placing correspondence on files kept in the pension divisions was introduced by Roland Wilkins in the 1920s. At that time different files existed for each pensioner's paid vouchers, which were stored in separate filing sections. These were closed down in the Second World War, and since the move to Crawley all paid vouchers have been stored centrally in the roll store. The issue and payment of every pension voucher was faithfully recorded in huge ledgers, which took loose-leaf form during Mr Wilkins's time and continued to strain the backs of all who lifted them until the computer system and a new-style file cover rendered them obsolete in 1975. Tax and voluntary deductions were among the details entered. The PGO has always been responsible for deducting income tax from pensions; until 1931 its staff also issued and checked tax returns and made assessments. Since the Pay As You Earn system began in 1944 the Office has used tax codes supplied by the Inland Revenue, a system which itself is shortly to be computerised. The first voluntary deductions were made in 1892, in respect of life insurance premiums, but the facility generally is still available only to civil service pensioners.

The only time that the service has been interrupted has been during industrial disputes or when pensioners found themselves in enemy countries or occupied territories in the Second World War, and even then the Office managed to arrange for payments to be advanced by United States diplomats before their nation, too, entered the war in 1941. The postal service to the Channel Islands was halted during the occupation of 1940-5, but many pensioners were assisted by their banks or the island authorities, which were reimbursed after the war. Since the war some pensioners in communist-controlled countries have experienced difficulties in negotiating PGO vouchers, and alternative arrangements have had to be made — sometimes involving payment to an agent or mail order company supplying food parcels in place of money.

Concern by both staff and management of the PGO for the welfare of the pensioners was demonstrated well by their efforts to obviate hardship during two post-war strikes. In 1971, the Post Office strike caused the suspension of all mail deliveries at a time when the PGO had 600,000 pensioners paid by voucher. Arrangements were made with the Department of Employment for local labour exchanges to act as collection points: for six weeks the PGO was transformed into a giant sorting office, as each batch of vouchers produced by the computer

PENSION SECTION 1985, at Sutherland House.
Photo: Ken Bridle.

was manually sorted into regions, towns and postal districts for delivery to regional employment centres. Many pensioners telephoned to arrange for them to collect their vouchers from the Crawley or Eagle House offices, while others living in Sussex and Surrey were surprised to have their pension delivered personally by PGO staff on their way home from work. Ten years later the same spirit of concern and helpfulness was in evidence when a national dispute over civil service pay caused the shutdown of the PGO computers for six weeks. This time staff co-operated in manually preparing and issuing more than 150,000 'emergency advances' to pensioners reporting hardship in response to press advertisements, and later had to obtain and account for repayments when the computers got back to work.

In the 1950s, before the discontinuance of cash payment an extremely close bond developed between the PGO and many of its pensioners. Some used to travel many miles to collect their payments; some became so well known that staff were concerned if they did not put in an appearance on payment day; some expressed gratitude for personal service by bringing in cakes and chocolates, leaving a shilling under the blotting paper or in one case bestowing a monthly blessing upon an embarrassed cashier. In many ways it is a pity that the service is unavoidably less personal now that the Office is physically remote from most of its pensioners, makes the majority of payments to banks, and has nearly 1,200,000 clients. Yet still the staff take a pride in the service they give in response to telephoned or written enquiries. Former Paymaster General Shirley

Williams recalls how she was impressed by the 'family' relationship which existed between section staff and their pensioners, and by the small number of complaints she received about the PGO's service. In their concern that pensioners should not be treated as mere reference numbers but as respected senior citizens the staff are constantly aware that one day they, too, will receive a pension from the PGO.

12. TECHNOLOGY : *evolution of the PANDA*

Early machines

In the earliest days of the PGO the only aids available to clerical staff were strictly non-mechanical, like the printed salary tables, which were in use from the 19th century right up to 1974, to assist the clerks in calculating periodic and broken period amounts from an annual rate of payment. The first record of a mechanical aid occurs in 1876, when we hear of the failure of trials with a copying machine (for making second copies of the detail entries of daily payments) because it proved too complicated for the staff to operate. Until the introduction of typewriters and the facility for carbon copying in the 1890s, the Office employed 'writers' to copy important letters, both incoming and outgoing, in longhand into bound correspondence registers. When permanent instructions to staff were issued, such as Sir Henry Parnell's 1841 regulations and Bartlett's Memorandum of 1898, they had to be printed by the Stationery Office; other notices and reminders were circulated in manuscript, to every employee if necessary. At first typewriters were used only for high level correspondence from senior officers, and it was not until 1919 that minutes of meetings, Office instructions and letters to pensioners began to be typed. By 1920 a stencil duplicator was in use to facilitate the distribution of instructions, in 1931 the Office had a spirit duplicator and by the 1960s a dyeline copier and a Verifax one-off photocopier. However, all of the department's forms were printed at the Stationery Office until the acquisition of the PGO's own offset litho printer in 1974.

At the beginning of the 20th century the first mechanical calculators were being introduced into offices. Although there is no record of precisely when they came into use in the PGO, it was probably soon after the Great War, to ease the impact of the unprecedented volume of transactions. The original Burroughs machines were large, heavy boxes with over 90 keys and a paper roll on which the amounts keyed were printed; a long lever at the side operated the mechanism which printed a total. Initially these 'add-listers' were used only in central machine rooms, where the amounts paid on pension vouchers and payable orders were listed in order to agree claims by the banks and to debit the relevant votes and subheads. In the 1930s a more sophisticated electrically-powered machine evolved. Operated by only the more experienced machinists, this incorporated a 'shuttle' device which made it possible for the reference number, net amount, tax and voluntary deductions on pension vouchers to be all listed simultaneously on one sheet. The sheets could then be 'read off' by other clerks against the pension ledgers as a secondary check against fraud or internal error. As the manually-operated listers were replaced by electric machines, the obsolete equipment found its way into the pension divisions, where it was used to total the tax payover to the Inland Revenue. However, for the clerks with the mundane tasks of preparing and issuing vouchers, and marking them off when paid, there was little relief until the mechanisation of pension payments which began in 1957. This was incredible in the light of the fact that in 1947 the Office had experimentally used punched cards as payable orders to aid the sorting and listing of ¼ million war damage claims issued by the Board of Trade, and moreover the experiment had been acknowledged as a success. Two years later a new machine class of grades first appeared, comprising senior machine operators (SMO), machine operators (MO) and machine assistants (MA) but these merely replaced the clerical grades on add-listing equipment in the detail and agreement sections.

Mechanisation of pensions

A mechanised pension system was needed badly, to remove monotony from the clerical duties and reduce the inconvenience to pensioners, banks and the Office itself, which was inherent in the existing manual procedures. In 1955 the PGO was paying 300,000 pensions, mostly by vouchers payable monthly or quarterly. Because of the need for variations in the wording to provide for different conditions of payment and for distinctive colours of paper to facilitate manual sorting, there were at least 150 different types of voucher. As a general rule, for pensions where no tax was deductible monthly vouchers were posted once a year, in batches of 12; for taxable cases vouchers were issued half-yearly because of the high incidence of code changes during a year. When a pensioner's batch of vouchers was exhausted, he was required to apply formally for a fresh supply. All vouchers were prepared by hand from the details on the pensioner's ledger sheet, and recorded on a 'fly sheet' within the ledger. The only mechanical aid was a rotary date stamp, the prototype of which had been invented and built at home by a young EO to simplify the preparation of vouchers in his own section: it was later produced by the Stationery Office for general use within the PGO.

Pensioners were supposed to sign and present each voucher on or after the payable date, but it was not unusual for an unscrupulous person to attempt to get payment early by cashing vouchers months before the due date. Such pensioners were designated 'one-ers' and thenceforth were sent only one voucher at a time, a step which penalised the Office as much as the payee because it created exceptions from the general rule. The method of deducting income tax also must have created confusion: for the first two vouchers in a quarter the Office made net advances of 8 per cent of the annual rate, and every third month carried out the necessary adjustment to correct the quarter's tax.

From branch banks the vouchers passed through the banks' clearing system to the PGO, where the total claimed was paid and machine-listed for subsequent agreement. Then each voucher was individually examined and, if acceptable, marked off as paid against the fly sheet record of its issue. After that came the read-off from the detail sheets. By tradition, monthly and quarterly pensions followed the general rule with salaries, in being paid on the last day of a calendar month or quarter (the sole exceptions being teachers, for whom in 1919 the Board of Education had devised the quaint system of payment according to birth dates). Thus for a week or so after the end of each month the banks and the Office were inundated with vouchers presented for payment, while for the rest of the month the staff had time on their hands.

There was also an inconvenient method of referencing pensions, consisting of a prefix denoting the division, followed by a service code and the pensioner's

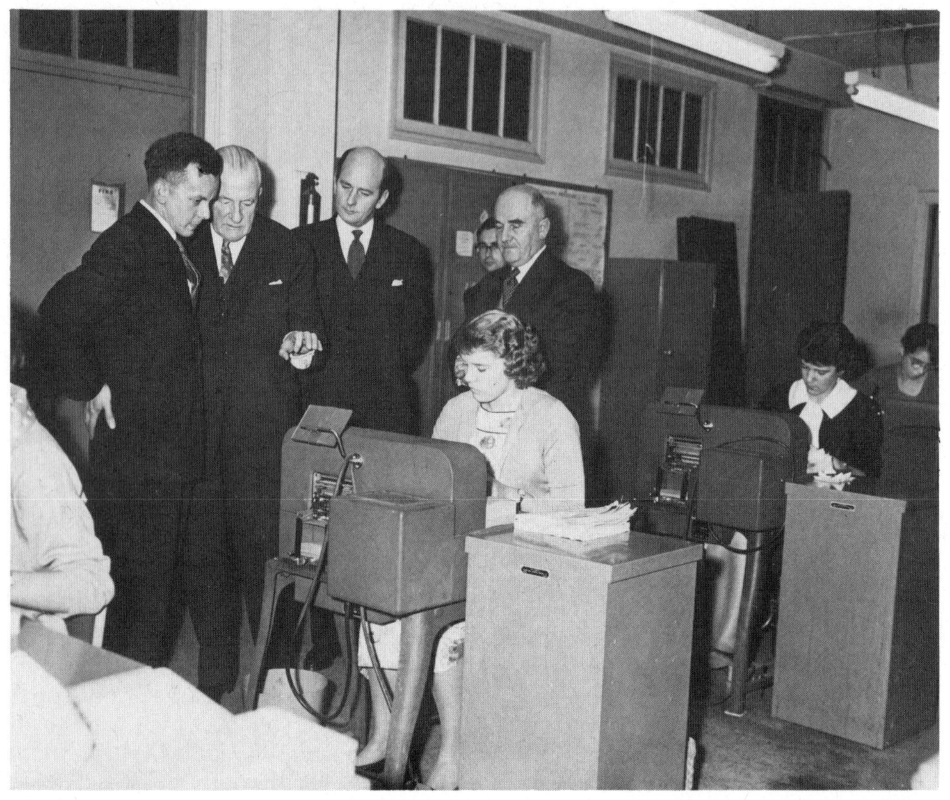

POWERS SAMAS PUNCHES at Russell Square House, 1960. Left to right in the inspection party are Norman Norfolk (Head of MD), Lord Mills (Paymaster General), Lord Mills's private secretary, Eric Webster (APG's private secretary) and John Vetch (Assistant Paymaster General).
Photo: Fox Photos Ltd, reproduced by permission of International Computers Ltd.

number. This resulted in a variety of types and lengths of reference ranging from 10D/NC12345 to 9D/RAFRP12345 and from 12D/234567 to 11D/SEX123456. As each division had its own card index of pensioners there was great difficulty in identifying correspondence in which, quite commonly, writers ignored the printed divisional prefix quoted on their pension vouchers. The system also created extra work when pensions were moved from one division to another — a regular practice in the three teachers' pensions divisions.

In spite of all these disadvantages the 'old guard' who ran the PGO in the early 1950s were rather wedded to traditional procedures, and had succeeded in resisting several Treasury attempts to introduce modern methods. The opportunity for change came with the arrival in 1955 of a new Assistant Paymaster General, Cyril West, who wasted no time in declaring his support for mechanisation. It would, he said, 'help to remove much of the drudgery from Clerical Officers' duties'. Shortly after Mr West's untimely death in the following year, the Treasury authorised a pilot scheme, with the object of proving once and for all that the PGO's pensions could and should be paid more efficiently. The scheme would involve mechanising the 30,000 war disability pensions in 10D, which had fewer taxable cases but a high incidence of rate changes. To implement it the Office looked to the man who as an EO seven years earlier had invented the invaluable rotary date-stamp. Norman Norfolk was appointed to 10D initially as an HEO but quickly became its head of division. He soon found that the type of system (40-column punched cards) had been decided already; however, after an intensive training course with the suppliers, Powers Samas Limited, he was equipped to steer the division through its pioneering project. The equipment was installed in the division in the spring of 1957. By May Mr Norfolk had completed his training of the clerical staff, appointed an SMO, 3 MOs and 2MAs to punch the cards and operate the machines, and supervised the conversion to punched cards of all the data needed to pay the first 7,000 pensions — the last remaining pensions of the Great War. By September the whole of 10D's pensions were on the new system.

The experiment was supported throughout by the Staff Side, once their early fears about redundancies had been allayed, and by October it had proved sufficiently successful for the Treasury to sanction its extension to all of the department's pensions. Further Powers Samas machinery was installed and more operators recruited, as one by one the work of all pension divisions was mechanised, with the chief exception of the pensions paid by weekly order book. In 1958 a new Mechanised Division (MD) was set up, headed by the well qualified Mr Norfolk, in order to centralise all machine work. By 1961, when the take-on was completed, MD employed an SMO, 4 MOs and 26 MAs.

The full range of Powers Samas equipment consisted of 'automatic' key punches with a facility for verification; sorters capable of processing 40,000 cards an hour (but requiring six passes to sort a six-digit reference); reproducers for making exact copies of cards and adding certain constant data; interpolators for comparing or merging cards; and tabulators for printing the vouchers. By the time teachers' pensions were mechanised MD possessed two more large, metal boxes called EMPs (electronic multiplying punches), to undertake the monthly calculation of income tax. The despatch of vouchers was mechanised also, the machinery comprising bursters, joggers, folders, inserters and a sensitive weighing machine. The new machines were heavy (the floors needed strengthening to carry their weight) and today would seem excessively large for their limited range of ability. Nevertheless, despite teething troubles and growing pains, the newest additions to the PGO workforce proved their worth and led the way to modern computer systems. At a stroke, they transformed the work of pension sections.

No longer did clerks have to address envelopes, prepare or check vouchers before issue, sort or mark them off when presented for payment, read off detail lists against the ledgers, or manually total the tax agreement and prepare the yearly P35/P60 statements of pensions and income tax. The system had other advantages. The number of different versions of pension voucher was reduced from 150 to 6, although this upset the widow of one naval officer when she started to receive vouchers coloured air force blue. The concentration of work just after the end of each month disappeared when the payment dates of most existing pensions were changed to the 5th, 10th, 15th, 20th, and 25th of the month (pensioners who protested were labelled 'last day objectors' and their dates left undisturbed). The system also provided an opportunity to introduce a standard referencing system, at the suggestion of another promising young EO, Eric Webster. Devised by Messrs Norfolk and Clay, the references each consisted of a letter and two numerals, indicating the pension service, subhead and control account, followed by three further numerals denoting the sequence within the account. For the first time, the term 'control' came into use to indicate pensions grouped together in order that clerical sections could keep a check on the mechanised accounts. Finally, mechanisation did result in staff savings of around 25 per cent, but the Office averted redundancies by staggering the take-on of pensions and allowing the slack to be taken up by normal wastage of staff and growth in pension numbers.

Computer

For tax calculation the EMPs were an improvement on the manual system, but they soon became archaic in comparison with the programmable electronic computers which were being developed in the early 1960s. In 1963 they were replaced by the Office's first computers, the ICT 558s. These two machines performed the task in a fraction of the time, although they required the installation of a reinforced floor and air-conditioning equipment, complete with humidifier and a bucket to catch the drips. They also needed programming, so firstly John Bell and later Diana Raban were trained to become the Office's first computer programmers. The 558s worked side by side with the remaining Powers Samas machinery until the final closure of MD in 1970.

Meanwhile Norman Norfolk was involved in the next step in the PGO's technological advance. In February 1962 he became part of a four-man investigation into the feasibility of an automatic data processing system at the PGO. The existing punched card equipment was expected to reach the end of its useful life by 1969, but the team quickly concluded that another punched card system would be too limited for the sort of improvements they had in mind. In a prophetic report of April 1963 the team foresaw the day when a multi-purpose PGO computer would be able to calculate and pay pensions increase, hold diary dates, perform accounting for income tax and voluntary deductions, print counterfoil notes, read the vouchers and payable orders presented for payment, produce weekly order books, agree bank claims, accept schedules from other departments in machine-readable form and carry out payment reconciliations. All of these prophecies came true eventually, although some of the tasks were not computerised until the early 1980s.

On the strength of this vision of the future, Mr Vetch at once set up a Computer Group (CG), consisting of a principal (Norman Norfolk), 2 SEOs, 4 HEOs and 2 EOs, to analyse existing procedures and assess their suitability for computerisation. After 18 months of fact-finding and meetings within the PGO, with other departments and with computer suppliers, CG (which by now had taken on and started training another 7 EOs) recommended that a large computer be set up at Crawley, capable of processing both pensions and banking work. Despite some reservations about alternative facilities in the event of a breakdown, the department's senior managers gave their support, and in January 1965 the Treasury approved capital expenditure up to £700,000. Tenders were invited from nine computer companies, and in April 1966 a contract was placed with English Electric Leo Marconi (later English Electric Computers Ltd) for a LEO 326 machine. Within weeks that firm announced the development of its System 4 range and persuaded the Office and its technical advisers that a better buy would be their System 4/50 model, which they would deliver by September 1967.

Now work began in earnest on the design and programming of the new

POWER SAMAS TABULATORS printing pension vouchers: Norman Norfolk shows them to Lord Mills and John Vetch, 1960.
Photo: Fox Photos Ltd, reproduced by permission of International Computers Ltd.

pensions and banking systems. It was decided early on that it would be unwise to attempt to introduce at once all of the potential changes to the pensions system, because of the volume of work involved, the shortage of available time, the lack of computer expertise within the PGO and the major upheaval of staff which was being caused by dispersal. Therefore the full pensions system would be introduced in stages. Stage I would be virtually a carbon copy of the punched card system, except that the contents of the 40-column cards would be transferred to magnetic tape or discs: as far as the pension sections were concerned the changeover would be invisible. Stage II, which would coincide with decimalisation, would simplify the input forms and begin computer calculation of pensions increase, while stage III would implement more radical changes once CG had acquired more experience and the pension divisions' staffing situation was more stable. On the other hand, the banking system was to be fully computerised as early as possible, in order to effect an early closure of the clerical and machining sections of FD in Russell Square House. The only clerical work left would be the handling of lump sum vouchers issued by the pension sections and the accounting work carried out by the book-keeping section.

In order to enlarge its team of programmers CG held 'QUIS' aptitude tests for existing PGO staff, recruited direct entrant EOs through the Civil Service Commission and between 1966 and 1969 bought the services of trained programmers from English Electric and borrowed experienced staff from the Inland Revenue, Worthing. Two of the new staff were the department's first blind programmers, who attended with their loyal guide dogs. All new programming staff were trained by the computer suppliers in the assembler language USERCODE and the high level language CLEO, which had been designed for the LEO range of computers but was adopted by the PGO for use on System 4/50s. The expected arrival of the computer in September 1967 necessitated other increases in the CG complement.

Early in April 1967 the first three operators were selected, and trained on a prototype System 4 machine at the company's headquarters; data preparation staff from the punch pool which had been set up in the Old Post Office were assigned and retrained; and input/output control clerks were chosen to serve as the interface between the computer and its users in the pension sections and customer departments. The computer, however, was late to arrive. Programmers had to send their work to the suppliers' headquarters for testing and the data preparation section gained experience in operating the new Datek paper tape punching machines by taking in work for local authorities, banks and other private companies.

Meanwhile the Office began a public relations exercise to inform the rest of its staff of the way in which their work would be affected by the computer, and to get it accepted as everyone's friend. A series of Computer Bulletins was started in 1967, and the staff were invited to participate in a competition to 'Name the Computer'. CG, it appears, were fed up with referring to it as 'it', and a prize of £2 2s. was offered for the best suggestion. The 76 entries revealed a range of attitudes to computerisation, from touching faith to downright distrust. Among the more flattering suggestions were ENOCH (Effective and Non-effective Orders, Competently Handled), CHLOE (Computer Helps Lessen Omissions and Errors) and ECCLES (Electronic Crawley Computer Leaves Eveyone Speechless), while GOD (General Order Data) and GAWD (Gear for Automatic Warrant Dispensing) were felt to be a trifle blasphemous. After ruling out the rather dubious acronyms CAMP (Computer for Automatic Mechanised Pensions) and COMPOST (Crawley Office for Machine Payments, Orders and STatistics), the judging panel finally opted for the cuddly image suggested by PANDA, the simple but appropriate abbreviation for Payments AND Accounts.

Well in time for the new systems, the pension voucher and payable order documents were redesigned to provide for magnetic ink encoding, so that they could be speedily read and sorted by the Burroughs cheque-reading machines on which the success of the computerised banking system depended. It was essential for the correct charging of accounts and matching of lodged orders and vouchers against the schedule details that only perfect account and serial numbers were input to the system. To achieve this a 'check digit' system was devised. Each number was extended to include an additional digit which bore a mathematical relationship to the preceding figures, and thus the computer would be able to check validity and reject for manual investigation any that failed the test. The system meant that when the payable documents were printed not only did the printer have to encode a row of figures and symbols at the bottom in magnetic ink, but two check digits had to be correctly calculated and printed at the same time. Mr Norfolk had great difficulty in persuading the printing trade and some of the departments that this was a feasible proposition, but his persistence paid off when at last he found a small but imaginative firm only a stone's throw from the new Crawley office which was prepared to find a way to meet the PGO's requirements. They succeeded, and in 1985 were still printing vouchers for the department. To aid the detection of input errors to the pensions system, check letters were added similarly to pension reference numbers.

At last, in June 1968, the long-awaited PANDA arrived from its Cheshire factory, the delivery coinciding with the merger of English Electric Computers with ICT to form International Computers Ltd (ICL). After exhaustive trials, the payment of pension vouchers began to be handled by the banking system in June 1969, but it was September 1970 before the pension issuing system was fully operational and October 1971 before the full take-on of payable order banking work. Both systems were successfully converted to decimalisation in February 1971.

During the early stages of the transfer of work to the computer it soon became evident that it was not handling the work at the predicted speeds. To enable the full range of work to be absorbed within three years it had been necessary to extend computer running time to two shifts (in November 1969), carry out much testing on similar computers at the Ministry of Transport, Swansea, and double the core size of PANDA from 128K to 256K bytes of storage in May 1970. In addition ICL installed a second ICL 4/50 computer with 128K bytes of storage in April 1971. The installation of a second PANDA and of standby generators in 1972 provided overdue standby facilities in the event of computer breakdown or power cuts. The combined configuration of the two PANDAs became 2 central processors, 2 operating consoles, 2 Magnetic Ink Character Recognition (MICR) cheque readers with speeds of 600 documents a minute, 12 exchangeable disc store drives, 19 magnetic tape decks, 4 paper tape readers, 3 80-column card readers and 3 printers with an effective speed of 1100 lines a minute. Input to the computers was by a variety of means. The daily bank lodgments were converted to magnetic tape after passing through MICR readers; the payable order schedules were received from different departments on magnetic tape, 80-column cards, paper tape or 'hard copy', which, like the input forms received from pension divisions, was punched on to paper tape by the data preparation section. In 1974-5 the Datek paper tape machines were replaced by CMC key-to-disc equipment, using visual display units.

The new banking system in particular, was a vast improvement on the labour-intensive clerical system of Russell Square days. Its most important new feature from the PGO point of view was the automatic marking-off of paid orders, which saved much time-consuming and tedious clerical work. The customer departments were spared a considerable manual chore by PANDA's ability to carry out a reconciliation of orders issued with those actually paid. Before that (except for a brief period during the Second World War) all payable orders accepted for payment by the PGO were returned to the departments. It took a laborious comparison of paid orders with ledger entries of issues to identify which issues had not been paid and which had exceeded the three month validity period. From 1970 the PGO was able to send to each department a monthly reconciliation statement and a detailed list of out of date orders. Both the Treasury and the Exchquer and Audit department showed commendable confidence in the new system by allowing the payment totals on PGO reconciliation statements to be treated as 'certified figures' for inclusion in the departments' appropriation accounts. From this time paid orders were retained in the Office instead of being returned to the customer departments: they were

COMPUTER HALL AT SUTHERLAND HOUSE, showing the ICL 2970 range of equipment (PANDAs 3 and 4).
Photo: Ken Bridle, 1985.

kept in the specially-constructed roll store exactly as presented by the banks, but could be located if required for scrutiny by means of a new 'clearing' suite of programs which held records of paid vouchers and orders for up to seven years after their issue. In 1975 the system was enhanced to allow microfilming of the cleared records.

The banking system's efficiency soon attracted new work from the Driver and Vehicle Licensing Centre, Ministry of Agriculture, Fisheries and Food and the Lord Chancellor's Department. Many Scottish departments had been drawing on the Queen's and Lord Treasurer's Rememberancer's (QLTR) office, using payable orders similar to those of the PGO. QLTR made substantial savings in 1971 by transferring all of this work to the PGO's new computerised system. By 1973 PANDA had also begun to process and account for credits received by the Crown and County Courts, using a new 'accounting' suite, the first to be documented according to the PGO's version of the National Computing Centre's technical and documentation standards.

The two PANDAs had been given a life expectancy of 10 years by their makers, so no sooner had they settled down to smooth, efficient running than it was time for Computer Branch (CB) — too big to be a 'Group' now, with over 200 staff — to begin considering their replacement. ICL were developing the 2900 range of computers, which seemed to suit the purposes of PGO, but the snag was that CLEO was now a dead language, and the whole of PGO's programs would have to be rewritten in the universal COBOL. Therefore the software bureau Leasco employed COBOL when writing the weekly pensions system: implemented in June 1975, this entailed the purchase of further advanced technology in the Bowë machine for producing weekly order books, and resulted in substantial clerical savings. Soon afterwards development began on another new system, APEX, which went into live operation in 1977.

After detailed investigations into future computer requirements, and with the approval of the Central Computer Agency, an order was placed in July 1975 for two of ICL's new 2970s. As the existing systems would need to be rewritten in COBOL, the opportunity was taken to plan for enhancements, including many of the features originally planned but shelved in the 4/50 pension systems, provision for the new payment method through BACS, and automatic production of printouts confirming action taken by the computer. In 1976-7 the Burroughs MICR readers were replaced by two IBM models, each with its own small computer, capable of detecting errors before they crept into the main system. The ICL computers, PANDA 3 and PANDA 4, arrived in 1977-8, but by the end of 1980 it had been found necessary to enhance the available power in order to process the PGO's time-critical work more efficiently, and the Office found itself with two models 2976 which were 'dualled' in 1982. The versatile computer then boasted 8 megabytes of main store, 4 store multiple access controllers, 22 disc store drives, 16 magnetic tape decks, 3 80-column card readers and 5 printers with effective speeds of 110 lines a minute.

Advances

The transfer of PGO systems to the new computers began in May 1978 with weekly pensions and was complete by July 1980. Once the last of the banking records had been cleared from the old computers the 4/50s were sent to the breaker's yard. Another new system made its debut on the 2976s: this was

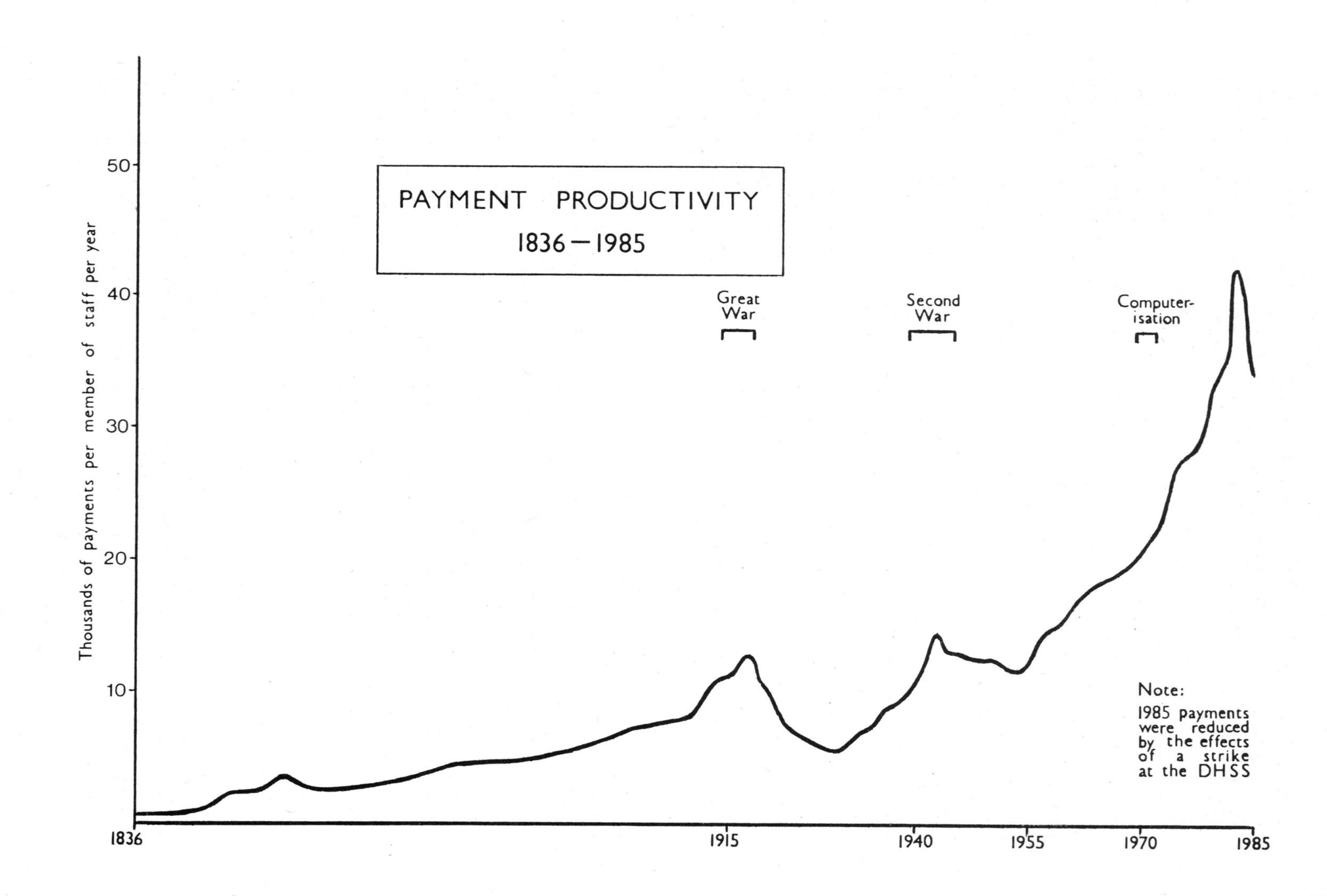

PAYMENT PRODUCTIVITY
1836—1985
Great War
Second War
Computer-isation
Note:
1985 payments were reduced by the effects of a strike at the DHSS
Thousands of payments per member of staff per year
50
40
30
20
10
1836
1915
1940
1955
1970
1985

designed to process GMP notifications from the DHSS at Newcastle, provided on magnetic tape, and to pass to the pension system those for which it already had a record. With the bread-and-butter systems safely on the 'mainframe', CB could begin to consider further improvements. Already the new systems had simplified the work of pension sections, which no longer needed to calculate periodic or broken period amounts — they simply input the annual pension rates to PANDA and the computer did the rest. Long-standing confusion between the pensions and banking systems was overcome by an 'interface' suite which enabled all input from pension divisions to be sent to one control section only. Also, some correspondence was obviated by the printing of brief counterfoil notes on vouchers or advices.

Soon afterwards PANDA could carry out accounting for income tax and voluntary deductions and report 'diary' reminders. A computerised index of pensioners was set up in 1983 to replace over a million index cards maintained in five different places. Visual display units appeared in pension divisions, in connection with the new index, and in 1984 microfiche readers were placed in every section when pension issue records were transferred to fiche. In 1984 also, teachers' pensions became the first to have new and amended awards sent by the awarding department on magnetic tape, which could be used by PANDA to make payments without clerical intervention. In 1983 the MICR readers became redundant when the Bank of England began to read the daily lodgment and send the details by tape to the PGO; in 1985 a financial management system was developed in accordance with the government's desire to see more accountability; and at long last the old-established book-keeping procedures are being computerised.

Advances in fields other than computer technology have been no less dramatic. In the typing pool electric typewriters were introduced in 1973, and in 1984 a word processor was installed to prepare and maintain the department's forms and instructions more economically. The MUFAX facsimile transmission link with the London caller office was established in 1971, and transferred to the Bank of England in 1980. In 1982 the Office was connected to the Government Telecommunications Network in order to save on the cost of telephoning and TELEXing other departments. 1985 saw the installation of sophisticated new despatch equipment to secure postal charge discounts by sending mail to the Post Office already sorted by postcodes. In a completely different field a voice alarm system (introduced in 1976), which allows messages to be broadcast to all parts of the Office, and the facility to use 'walkie talkie' transmitters (available since 1982) have made the Office a safer place to work in the event of emergencies.

The technological advances of the last 25 years have indeed had a substantial impact on the department. In general the staff have welcomed rather than tolerated the changes, for jobs are more varied and satisfying since the elimination of the repetitive chores of pre-mechanisation days, and the opportunity now exists for those with the right aptitude to move into the new and challenging areas of computer systems, programming and operations. Technology has enabled the Office to reduce the ratio of staff to pensions and payments, but a four-fold growth in the volume of work undertaken has averted the spectre of redundancy. The spectacular growth rate has not been entirely fortuitous, for in many cases it was the increased efficiency which attracted the additional work — which, in turn, increased the efficiency still further.

As CB begin to plan for the next computer systems, developments in telecommunications and other fields indicate that the pace of change will accelerate, and there is every prospect of an even better service to pensioners, customer departments and the PGO staff.

13. PEOPLE : *staff matters*

Paymaster General

In this chapter on the people of the PGO and the events which have affected their numbers, duties and working conditions, it is perhaps proper to start at the top, and consider the changing role of the Paymaster General himself. During the earliest years of the Office (1836 to 1852) the Minister held no other appointment, and therefore was able to devote much time to devising and personally supervising the department's original regulations. Even the arch-critic Lord Monteagle had to admit that Sir Henry Parnell 'felt his responsibility and performed his duties'. However, in 1852 the post began to be held jointly with other Ministerial appointments, and at once the PGO was relegated to the back seat, with day to day control passing formally to the Assistant Paymaster General under power of attorney, while the Minister attended to more pressing duties. Monteagle commented caustically:

> *The Office of Paymaster General is at present only nominal — a mere sinecure — no salary is paid, but this remuneration is fully equal to the services rendered.*

The Select Committee of 1856 agreed with him that things were hardly satisfactory, and actually recommended that the Paymaster General should cease to be a political officer and become the 'acting and efficient head of the Pay Office, performing his duties in person'. No action was taken on this, and in 1874 a further report observed that because he was in charge of another public office and was not paid to perform the job of Paymaster General, the Minister was 'loth to undertake any business connected with it and it almost seems an intrusion to trouble him with any'. As a result, Stephen Cave was relieved of his post as Judge Advocate General in 1875, to become a full-time Paymaster General. It was not until the Great War that the Minister again had to divide his time between the PGO and other responsibilities, but gradually he became less and less involved in the Office's staffing and procedural problems.

In the 20th century it has become usual for the post to be filled by a senior politician with other, more time-consuming duties. For example, John Boyd-Carpenter (1962-4) had responsibility for the relocation of government offices, Shirley Williams (1976-9) was simultaneously Secretary of State for Education and Science, and Francis Pym (1981) was both Leader of the House of Commons and Chancellor of the Duchy of Lancaster. Cecil Parkinson (1981-3) and John Gummer (1984 to date) have each held the title in parallel with the chairmanship of the Conservative party. Occasionally the Paymaster General has had no other specific Ministerial post, but has been responsible for a non-departmental function such as government publicity, or, as in the last war, 'duties of a secret nature'. Each Minister also has traditionally held several simultaneous appointments *ex-officio*, including those of Chairman of the Commissioners and Treasurer of the Royal Hospital, Chelsea; Chairman of the

Commissioners of the Duke of York's School, Dover; and trusteeship of several charitable funds.

Strangely enough, the Paymaster General has no responsibility for the PGO's banking and pensions policies, which lie with Treasury Ministers. His sole duty with regard to the PGO is to see that the Office meets its obligations as agent for other departments, and although this involves him occasionally in parliamentary questions or correspondence with fellow MPs, it is generally delegated to the Assistant Paymaster General under the power of attorney which a new Minister signs immediately on taking office. The functions of the Paymaster General and his Office have long been a source of mystery, misunderstanding and even amusement among opposition MPs and the media, who become confused by the non-departmental duties which are often attached to the post. The appointment of George Wigg (1964-7) as Paymaster General with responsibility for government security brought a typically ill-informed attack from a west-country newspaper, which complained that the public were allowed to know little of his new role:

> *but we do know that he has roughly 700 civil servants to help him do it . . . Perhaps he thinks up awkward questions for Mr Wilson to put to all his other advisers . . . but does he really need 700 civil servants to do this?*

As might be expected the Minister's duties as Paymaster General are 'less than onerous', as one recent post-holder put it, and on the four occasions when the post has been left vacant (most recently for a period of 15 months in 1983-4), the effect on the Office has been negligible. The Minister's private office is no longer within the PGO but in the Cabinet Office in Whitehall. The Paymaster General therefore does not come into daily contact with the department, and the frequency of visits is dependent on the extent of other responsibilities. Nevertheless the title, with its long history, is proudly held. Cecil Parkinson, for one, was irritated when, in connection with his cabinet responsibilities, the media referred to him as party chairman rather than Paymaster General.

The Office, in turn, is proud to have had as its Minister many persons with international reputations. One of them, Neville Chamberlain (1923), went on to become Prime Minister, and many others have held senior cabinet rank. In recent years Reginald Maudling (1957-9) became an outstanding Home Secretary, and Viscount Eccles (1970-3) had been a pioneer of educational reform and post-war trade with Russia, while Francis Pym earned distinction as Foreign Secretary during the Falklands conflict of 1982. Shirley Williams subsequently became a founder of the Social Democratic party and in 1984 was elected as its first president.

35 Paymasters General were peers of the realm at the time of their appointment, and many others achieved that recognition afterwards. Many may have known little or nothing about the PGO before taking office, but by the time they left had developed respect and even affection for their little department and its staff.

Numbers and grades

In 1848 William Anderson had claimed:

to transfer to the Office business of an analagous kind will save the expense of an additional staff of superintending officers, paymasters and book-keepers; for our Office is very much like a banker's; a few thousand additional accounts give no great additional trouble to those who have to superintend it, because the business is conducted according to fixed regulations, which are applicable to a large as well as to a small number of payments.

The truth of these remarks has been borne out by events, for although there has been a seven-fold increase in staff at the PGO since its formation in 1836 this has been only a fraction of the growth in transactions. The advent of mechanisation and computer technology in particular has enabled the Office to take on considerable amounts of new work without a commensurate increase in personnel.

	Payments	*Pensions*	*Personnel*
1836	100,000 est	10,000 est	112
1885	380,000	25,000 est	78
1935	2,400,000	150,000	301
1955	7,500,000	310,000	619
1970	13,000,000	520,000	683
1985	30,000,000	1,200,000	837
Growth 1836-1985	× 300	× 120	× 7.5

In order to achieve such a phenomenal increase in the productivity rate per person the Office has undergone many internal changes during its 150 year span, changes which have had a profound effect on the duties and working conditions of everyone, from the Assistant Paymaster General to the lowest paid member of staff.

In contrast to the Ministerial post, which has seen 81 occupants in 150 years, there have been only 18 permanent heads of the PGO. The Assistant Paymaster General, now grade 5 (assistant secretary) has been accountable since at least 1867 for civil superannuation expenditure, and since 1978 fully responsible for the Office's administration costs also. To assist him is a small group of senior managers, at present two grades 6 (senior principal) and six principals, formerly chief clerks and principal clerks. Between 1942 and 1978 one of the senior principals bore the title Deputy Assistant Paymaster General, and for about 50 years before that, one of the principals received an allowance (£100 in 1896 which had risen to £105 by 1942) for deputising in the Assistant Paymaster General's absence. The second senior principal was added in 1972, with the upgrading of the post of head of CB.

Throughout its history the PGO's backbone has been formed by the executive and clerical grades, now part of the administration group of the civil service. The original senior clerks became first class clerks and by 1920 were being styled heads of division, or SEOs; senior examiners, or HEOs, were introduced only in 1890; while the present-day EOs were entitled assistant, junior and second class clerks in Victorian times and junior examiners from 1890 to 1956. The higher grades of the executive class always have been primarily supervisors, but the duties of the EO grade formerly revolved around chiefly examination and checking of vouchers and claims. When pension payment was mechanised, EOs became mainly checkers of forms prepared by COs, with a small managerial function. The present role of pension section EOs as first line managers with only limited checking responsibilities dates from the first round of staff inspections in 1969-74.

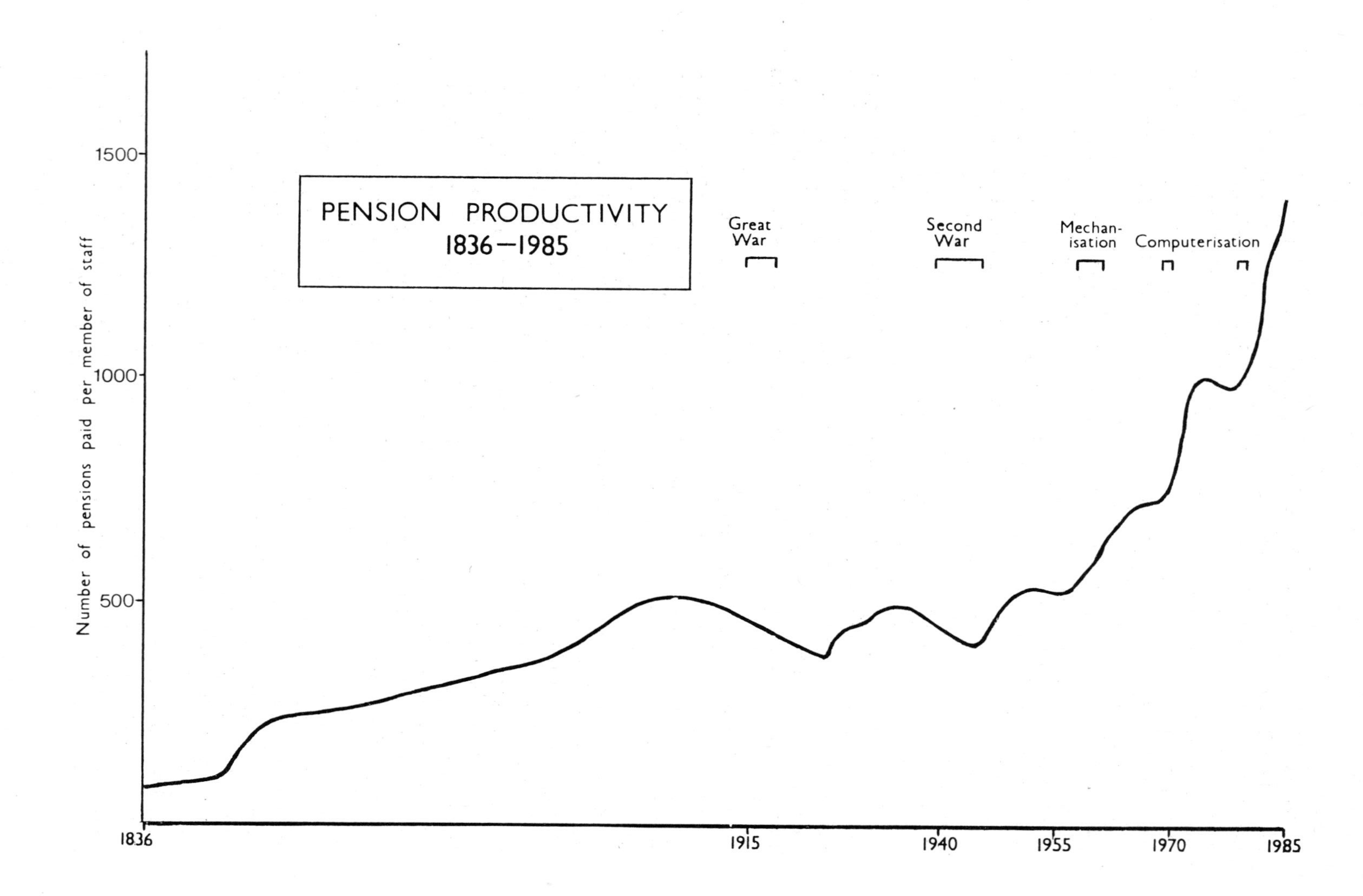
PENSION PRODUCTIVITY
1836—1985
Great War
Second War
Mechan-
isation
Computerisation
1500
1000
500
Number of pensions paid per member of staff
1836
1915
1940
1955
1970
1985

Today's COs originate from the 'lower division' of the civil service, set up in 1876; they became clerical officers in the reorganisation of 1922. The Victorian copyists or writers were originally not on the Office complement as their appointments were very temporary, but in 1876 they were first allowed to be promoted and established in the clerical class. In 1922 they became writing assistants, and acquired additional duties as CAs in 1936. Between the wars pension sections consisted usually of 3 or 4 COs, overseen by an EO, while the CAs (or writing assistants) were used mostly on general divisional duties such as maintenance of the filing system and the card index of pensioners. From 1970, however, CAs were given specific pension section duties and the standard pattern became 4 COs and 1 CA, managed by an EO.

Of the ancillary grades (the 'inferior persons' of Parnell's day) only the office keeper and messengers have been in the complement continuously since 1836. The post of housekeeper disappeared in 1838, and the charwomen, housemaids and cleaners in 1940, when the Whitehall office was vacated. Typists made their debut around 1894, paperkeepers in 1950, photoprinters and security officers in 1974 and telephone switchboard operators in 1980 (taking over a service run by the Post Office). The machine class, introduced in 1949, were regraded data processors (DPs) and senior data processors (SDPs) in 1976, in recognition of the new skills required to operate computer equipment, while the coming of computers also heralded new titles for specialist executive staff — programmers and systems analysts (1963), computer operators (1967) and project leaders (1970).

Over the years the PGO complement has been supplemented often by temporary help. During the world wars temporary clerks were needed because of the depletion of regular staff and the influx of extra work. Since the 1939-45 war students and other casual staff have been engaged to help with pensions increase work (before computerisation), the summer peak of teachers' retirements (until direct transfer of awards to the computer) and the processing of repayments after the 1981 strike. The Office has had also assistance from technical consultants during the development of its successive computer systems.

Organisationally there have not always been 'divisions' as we know them today. The port branches of 1836 were virtually self-contained units, but from 1837 at Whitehall both effective and non-effective work was performed in the same sections. By 1860 the Whitehall establishment was grouped into five distinct branches under the supervision of chief clerks, but the staff were appointed to 'rooms' rather than branches, and it seems that the chief clerks had little control over the allocation of duties. The segregation of effective from non-effective work began just after the Great War, and in 1926 Roland Wilkins assigned divisional numbers to distinct blocks of work. These were changed to the present system of meaningful titles in 1963, but since then there have been further amalgamations and sub-divisions. In 1970 CB was divided into functional commands under SEO project leaders, and in 1976 EOD was split into three units, Management Services (MS), Office Services (OS) and Personnel Services (PS), each also headed by an SEO.

Appointment and promotion

Before 1855 there was no consistency between government departments in the way they recruited new staff: each one had its own rules. When the PGO was set up the Treasury reserved the right of appointment to only the top five posts, but from the 1848 consolidation the Office was allowed to recruit no-one without Treasury sanction. However, with only 20 junior clerks and a minimal staff turnover recruitment must have been a rare event.

Applicants for clerical jobs at the PGO had to sit an examination (under the supervision of the Assistant Paymaster General) in arithmetic — including the calculation of interest and the purchase of stock and exchange — handwriting, dictation and precis from official documents. All results were referred to the Paymaster General, who could accept successful candidates on a year's probation. During that year the probationer had to pass an examination in book-keeping, and finally reports as to his 'talents, conduct and assiduity' were passed to the Minister, who had the power to dismiss the failures but had to forward the names of successful probationers to the Treasury Lords. Theirs was the responsibility for obtaining character references, before confirming an appointment. The minimum age of entry was 16, which in 1855 the Assistant Paymaster General felt to be 'decidedly too young'.

> *At that early age young men are found to pass at once from school to the office without any practical knowledge whatever, and too frequently from schools where writing and arithmetic are but little, if at all, attended to.*

On the other hand, 25 was apparently the upper age limit, beyond which 'persons could hardly be admitted with advantage to the Public Service or with comfort to themselves'. At that time all vacancies in the higher grades were filled by promotion, and before a clerk could be established he had to demonstrate that 'as he advances to the highest situations in the Office he will be fit to fill them efficiently'.

In 1855 standard civil service entry examinations were introduced, but still the Treasury made all appointments in the PGO. To the astonishment of the Paymaster General in 1865 the Treasury even claimed the right to appoint people to the messenger grades, accusing earlier Ministers of having 'improperly exercised the right of appointment'. The matter came to a head in that year over a vacancy in the post of office keeper. The Paymaster General had appointed Mr Fagg, a PGO messenger, but the Treasury wanted to fill the vacancy from their own ranks. Eventually the matter had to be referred for arbitration to Prime Minister Lord Russell, who sided with the Treasury. The unfortunate Mr Fagg was stripped of his promotion and the official apartments where he was living, but after representations from all of the PGO's senior officers about Fagg's zeal, efficiency and good conduct the Treasury graciously allowed him to keep the wages he had earned while office keeper.

Because of its small size and low staff turnover in the 19th century the Office could afford to be very selective in the engagement of new probationers, and resented the Treasury's growing practice of allowing entry by unrestricted competiton without regard to social status. In 1869 the Paymaster General, Lord Dufferin and Clandeboye, warned that this 'could not fail to make the Establishment a mixture of persons of very various social positions', a prospect which clearly filled him with horror. In his Lordship's opinion 'the emoluments of this Department are sufficiently attractive to obtain a plentiful supply of well qualified candidates from the families of Persons belonging to the liberal professions' and it would be wise to decline 'Persons of a lower grade'. In evidence given to the Civil Service Inquiry Commission of 1874 these views were echoed by the Assistant Paymaster General:

The difficulties which by reason of varieties of opinion and of tempers are at present experienced by those who have to keep Public Offices in a state of efficient co-operation are often great, notwithstanding the general similarity in the social position of the men who compose them; but if to these were superadded the jealousies and bitterness which would be sure to prevail if men doing the same duties were of all varieties of birth and connection, the loss to the Public from the impossibility of well fitting together such a body for the dispatch of business would be very great, and the occasional derangements frequent.

The clerks themselves were none too happy, either. They foresaw the division of the Office into 'superiors and inferiors', with the higher grades coming from an exclusive literary or social caste who knew less than their subordinates about the work of the department and found office routine repugnant, while the bulk of the staff who, 'however meagre their attainments and salaries' would be doing the work, would be 'deficient in culture' and disenchanted at the slim prospect of advancement. Despite such opposition, open competition continued. In 1881 even the door porters had to be examined in dictation and arithmetic, and immediately after each of the world wars special examinations were devised for those returning from active service or who had been deprived by the war of the chance of establishment. In 1912 the Treasury at last allowed the PGO to recruit messengers and porters, but it was not until the 1970s that the Office was empowered to appoint clerical staff. In that decade open competition was discontinued as a means of entry to the clerical grades, and replaced by the alternative methods of short answer tests or academic qualifications combined with interview. In the early 1980s the 'limited' examinations to CO and EO grades were abolished also, but the EO open competition is still available to serving COs. In practice the majority of EO examination successes assigned to the Office by the Civil Service Commission are people with computer aptitude or a proven record as COs in the PGO.

The PGO's early sensitivity over entitlement to pensions was mirrored in its quest for accuracy and prevention of internal fraud. All issues and payments were checked meticulously in the Victorian period, and if an overpayment was made the checker was held responsible and asked to repay. In 1962 one examiner appealed against such a ruling in a case involving £6 19s. 9d. which he had overpaid to the widow of a coastguard pensioner. The Treasury rejected the appeal, stating that it was 'the rule of all Offices in which public money is disbursed that the Officer entrusted with the responsibility of a payment is held accountable for any error committed in the payment'. In a similar case in 1870, two examiners were told to repay at the rate of £2 a month unless an overpayment was recovered from the payee. The seriousness with which the PGO took itself is well illustrated in an instruction of 1869:

The younger gentlemen of the Office . . . must not feel hurt or surprised if the general character of their private life is regarded as a matter of public concern. That pecuniary honesty should consist with a dissolute life cannot, as a general rule, be considered as probable; nor could it be safe to place important trust in persons reduced by extravagance to extreme need of money. Yet opportunities for fraud are here so general, and a necessity of withholding trust from any individual would entail so much inconvenience, that all who are employed must be trusted. It is therefore indispensable that all should be trustworthy.

In the 1870s the punishment inflicted upon persons who were intoxicated on

ROLAND WILKINS, CB, Assistant Paymaster General 1924-35.
Photo: R C S Taylor's album.

duty ranged from signing the pledge to loss of seniority, downgrading and even suspension from duty, while in 1880 a member of staff was dismissed for owing £5 to the luncheon club. During the regime of Roland Wilkins the names of checkers who had made serious mistakes would be reported so that their offences could be circulated to the whole Office. Although it is no longer the practice to recover overpayments from the checker responsible for an error, the PGO continues to place great emphasis on a consistently high standard of accuracy and integrity. Through quality control by line management in pension divisions and continual monitoring by the National Audit Office, the PGO's Internal Audit team and the Financial Control and Security Committee the Office is able to check that the required standards are being achieved.

When the Office was created the Treasury determined that promotions between the classes would be made on the basis of merit and good conduct, with seniority being given 'due weight'. Their Lordships directed also that clerks in 'embarrassed pecuniary circumstances' would be ruled out on the grounds that if they could not handle their own affairs they could not be trusted with those of a financial office. In the 19th century the Office complement was small enough for a regular reporting system to be unnecessary: if and when a vacancy occurred reports were called for, and a recommendation made to the Treasury. However, that was by no means the end of the matter, for the Treasury often decided not to appoint the PGO's nominee but someone from another department, and although in 1896 an assurance was given that the Office would have its fair share of promotions the second division clerks pointed out in 1903 that none had received a promotion for 25 years.

The reorganisation which took place in 1922 after the Great War expansion gave the PGO no less than 21 promotions to senior examiner and higher positions, and soon afterwards the Office was allowed freedom to confirm its own promotions. Between the wars, however, promotions once more became rare because managers were comparatively young and resignations almost unknown. Therefore the annual reporting system which developed in the 1920s as a result of pressure from the newly-formed Staff Side was a largely academic exercise, and the setting up of a seniority list only drew attention to the unfortunate position in which the junior staff found themselves. Until the 1950s all staff reports were completed by heads of divisions, who came in for frequent criticism for failing to consult their EOs. Reports on clerical staff were not delegated to HEOs until 1955, and it was another 11 years before responsibility finally passed to the EOs. In 1966 also, HEOs were first permitted to report on their EOs. Until the adoption of a standard, service-wide report form in 1955 reports consisted of percentage markings for each of the necessary attributes. This was never entirely satisfactory, and although Leonard Cuthbertson attempted to define requirements more precisely in 1941, it seems that reporting officers were making life very difficult for the promotion board. Apparently there was 'notable reluctance' to assign less than 99% for zeal and conduct, and it was necessary to remind the SEOs that even a 95% marking would 'carry no reflection'. However, a serious view might be taken of markings below 80%, for although they may be due to inexperience, temperament or personal characteristics difficult to correct, 'they begin to indicate ground for criticism'.

Promotion prospects improved considerably with the growth of work and staff complement occasioned by the Second World War, but as late as 1961 a CO could not be promoted before the age of 28, and then only with seven years' seniority. Later these conditions were gradually relaxed, and since 1980 the seniority required has been three years, with no age limit. EOs must now have four years' seniority in their grade before entering the field for HEO promotion, a far cry from the 1930s when men with 20 years' service as EOs had virtually no hope of getting further. In 1951 a promotion board was set up, consisting of the Establishment Officer and two principals. However, it was another eight years before EOs had to attend an interview before being promoted. In 1960 a 'short list' system emerged, and with it the provision for appeal against non-inclusion. In the 1970s four separate boards were created to recommend promotions to SEO, HEO, EO and the lower grades.

To help the department to make the best use of its resources, enhance job satisfaction and improve communications between management and staff, annual job appraisal reviews were initiated in 1971 and career development interviews three years later. A first step towards open reporting began at the end of 1978 with the disclosure of certain markings when requested by the reportee. Many staff now have the opportunity to prove their worth in a higher grade by substituting for their supervisor during absences. This had been allowed for long periods of sickness since early this century, but despite a Staff Side request in 1965 for automatic substitution to cover leave absences by EOs it was not until 1976 that this was agreed, initially on a trial basis in CS2 division.

Pay and hours

Before the 20th century evolution of national pay scales for the civil service, any increases were won only by convincing memorials from aggrieved staff to the Treasury, which held the purse-strings then as it does today. In the department's first 100 years it seems that there were few victories. In 1836 the lowest grade of clerk in the PGO started at £80 a year and progressed by £10 increments to £180. In 1936 the starting point for COs was £85, although after 21 years of satisfactory service in the same grade they could earn £350 a year. Female staff and people outside London earned even less. Between the wars, salaries fluctuated according to supposed variations in the cost of living and on some occasions were reduced, to the dismay of those affected. Since the 1960s, however, salaries have risen steadily, but not always in step with either the cost of living or pay rates in the private sector, a fact which has embroiled the PGO in national one-day strikes called by the civil service trade unions since 1973, and longer stoppages in the computer and other areas in 1979 and 1981.

Until 1867 salaries were paid quarterly in arrear, but then the Paymaster General sanctioned monthly payment 'knowing as I do that there are few more active causes of extravagance and consequent difficulties among clerks than the habit of getting into debt, which is almost forced upon them by the practice of paying their salaries at long intervals'. In 1959 the Office began to pay salaries direct to bank accounts on request, and in 1972 the PGO payroll was taken over by the Chessington Computer Centre.

One feature of life at the PGO has been the existence of various special allowances for performing certain duties. When the Office had its outstations in far away places like Hanover, Dublin and Chatham, clerks were paid allowances ranging from £70 to £100 to cover removal and travelling expenses; for undertaking the occasional duty at Woolwich dockyard a London clerk would receive 7s. 6d. (37½p) a trip, while a messenger was paid only 2s. 6d. For assessing income tax the Inland Revenue at first paid the Office a sum proportionate to the tax collected, but this unwise incentive was withdrawn in 1851 in favour of a fixed sum of £1,400, to be divided among the staff concerned. This was replaced in 1873 by a straight 8 per cent addition to their salaries, but only four years later new pay scales were introduced which were said to incorporate the allowances for the work. Because of the vast sums of cash for which they were responsible the PGO's cashiers in London and Dublin were granted risk money from 1860 and 1872 respectively. The London man's allowance of £30 a year was increased to £50 in 1895, rose temporarily to £75 for the duration of the Great War, and was abolished in 1937 when it, too, was absorbed in a new pay scale. Before dispersal PGO staff enjoyed also a London weighting allowance to reflect the higher cost of working in London, but after the move to Crawley this was retained by relocated staff only while they remained in the same grade.

Today, allowances are received by computer specialists, shift workers, and typists with special skills in audio, shorthand, typing and word processor operation. In 1863 a gratuity was paid to the PGO's office keeper and messengers to celebrate the marriage of the Prince of Wales, but true to the contemporary minute directing that this was not to be taken as a precedent for any similar occasions, there was no such commemoration of the royal wedding in 1981.

Working hours and annual leave allowance were further areas where each department went its own way in the 19th century. The PGO began life on a six hour working day (10 to 4), six days a week. The Paymaster General had

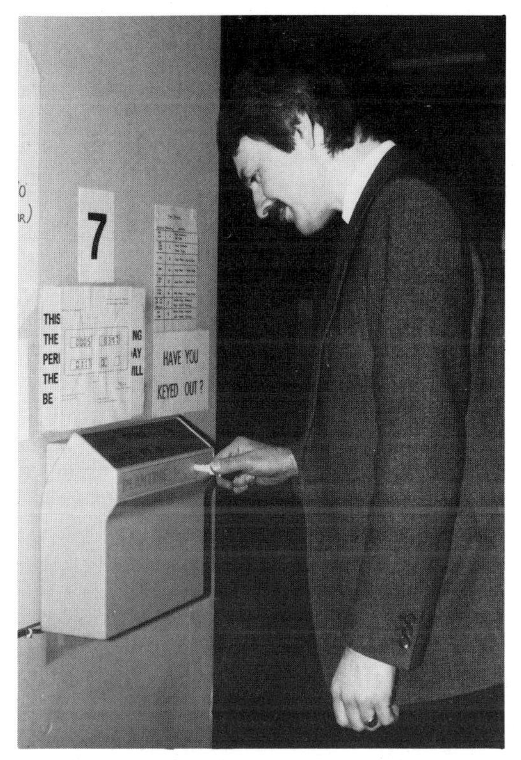

KEYING IN, 1985: the automatic flexible working hours equipment.
Photo: Ken Bridle.

discretion to grant a month's leave each year 'to such persons as he shall consider deserving of the indulgence', and he could extend this to six weeks if clerks had given extra time during the year and had displayed 'more than ordinary zeal and diligence'. By 1890 wide variations existed between the grades. First division officers (EOs and above) received up to 48 days — ie eight weeks — leave after 10 years' service, whereas newly-recruited lower division clerks (COs) were allowed only 14 days.

In 1868 the Office began to grant half of the staff unofficial absence after 2 pm on Saturdays, but it was not until 1925 that it was able to close officially on Saturday afternoons. Meanwhile the working day had been extended to seven hours (10 to 5) in 1896. There was some compensation for Saturday working in the comparatively generous leave allowances of the early 20th century: all grades down to HEO could earn 48 days leave, while EOs could receive 36 days, COs 24 days, typists 21 days and writing assistants 18 days. There was a ban, however, on all leave during the busy first eight days of each quarter. During both world wars staff were expected to put in extra hours for no additional pay, and by 1942 the standard working week had reached 49 hours. After that there was a steady reduction until, in 1956, when a five day week was introduced, the working week was set at 42 hours (including lunch). At the same time there was a lowering of leave allowances for all new staff. While the dispersal exercise was in progress the working week in London was further reduced, to 41 hours, but staff moving to Crawley had to revert to the national 42 hour week.

The first element of flexibility in attendance hours occurred in 1912, when some clerks were permitted to work from 9 to 4, provided that the Office remained staffed until 5 pm. In 1960 staff were invited to choose between 8.15 - 4.45 and 8.30 - 5 (earlier on Fridays) but an attendance book had to be signed on arrival, as it had since 1836. However, once the Office had become established in Crawley the time was right to abolish attendance books and introduce the flexible working hours (FWH) system which operates today. After brief experience with a manual system, proposals were put to the staff in an Office-wide referendum in 1975 for an automatic system, operated by each person keying in and out. The idea was then supported by only a small majority (335 votes to 330), but when the Plantime equipment was installed at the end of 1976 it proved universally popular and has undoubtedly added to the benefits of working at the PGO.

Whitleyism

The development of the FWH system was just one fairly recent example of co-operation between management and staff through the machinery of the PGO's Departmental Whitley Council (DWC). This was initiated in 1919, in accordance with national recommendations. The Assistant Paymaster General minuted:

> *The object of the Council is to secure the greatest measure of co-operation between the Administrative Head of the Department, as representing the State in its capacity as employer, and the staff in their capacity as employees, to provide machinery for dealing with grievances and generally to bring together the experience and different points of view respecting conditions of service within the Department.*

From the outset the Staff Side comprised representatives of every grade in the PGO, including, from 1925 to 1949, a delegate of the ex-servicemen from the Great War. The DWC has operated continuously and with much effect since 1919, apart from a four year break in the 1930s. The autocratic leadership and disciplinary methods of Roland Wilkins had led to much controversy and resentment which came to a head at two stormy DWC meetings in 1931. Having received no satisfaction for their grievances the Staff Side enlisted the aid of a national union official, and when he also failed to budge Mr Wilkins from his stance the Staff Side formally withdrew their representation on the DWC, a step which was endorsed shortly afterwards at a packed meeting of union members in a room at Central Hall, Westminster. There were only three dissenters. The DWC did not resume business until the appointment of James Mahood as Assistant Paymaster General in 1935.

The seating arrangements at DWC meetings were guaranteed to instil a sense of inferiority among the Staff Side. The Official Side sat in isolation and comparative comfort behind a large mahogany table, while the Staff Side were obliged to sit on hard, upright chairs with nothing but their laps on which to rest their papers. It was Cyril West who first arranged in 1955 for both sides to meet around the same table. During early years the DWC met up to four times a year, but since 1960 it has become usual for the full Council to meet only once a year, leaving sub-committees and personal discussion to iron out day to day problems and ease the passage of potential changes. Staff training, the suggestions scheme (started in 1948), staff inspections, health and safety, accommodation, new technology, financial management: these are just some of the topics which are now the theme of DWC sub-committees. In 1980 the Staff Side followed its national counterpart in becoming restyled the 'Trade Union Side' of the DWC.

Instruction

In the earliest days of the PGO all training took place at the newcomer's own desk, and written instructions were few and far between. All that the staff had were Treasury minutes relating to Office procedures and Parnell's regulations of 1841. Handwritten instructions were prepared in 1863 and 1870 which apparently had to be read, initialled and memorised. Bartlett's printed and bound Memorandum appeared in 1898 and was reprinted with amendments at least twice by 1910, but no definitive, comprehensive instruction was issued for another 38 years. The gap was partly filled by Wilkins's system of *ad hoc* Office instructions, notices and Establishment minutes which began in 1925, and a printed paperback booklet by principal clerk Arthur Carwithen which was published in 1927 under the snappy title 'Memorandum dealing with the supply of funds required by the Paymaster General for the purpose of paying for the public services of the various departments of the State, excluding the revenue departments'. This was updated by principal David Wheble in 1962, when it was renamed 'The Finance Work of the Paymaster General's Office'.

In the 1950s specialised divisional instructions began to appear, and in 1964 guides to the pension work of the Office were issued to reflect the changes brought about by mechanisation and the 558 computer. Named Penguide and Taxguide, they were replaced in 1971 by Compendium, the first manual for the new computerised pension system at Crawley, and this in turn gave way in 1980 to a new Penguide describing the more sophisticated system of the ICL 2900 computers. Today there are coloured supplements to Penguide which relate to divisional variations from the general rules, necessitated by differences in the pension schemes. In 1976 the first job description, for pension HEOs, was published; since then job descriptions have been devised for almost every post in the Office.

With the prospect of an influx of new staff just after the 1939-45 war, the Controller of Office Services was given responsibility in 1949 for central training in the PGO, and two years later HEOs were first appointed as divisional training officers. However, the impetus then waned, apart from a flurry of activity around the time when new staff were being recruited prior to dispersal. For a short period after the move to Crawley central training went through another quiet period, staffed by only 1 HEO and an EO tutor who was also clerk of stationery. The present comprehensive training programme which provides for general introductory training for all new entrants and specialised courses for the more experienced staff dates only from the 1970s, when the central training section was reconstituted with a complement of 1 HEO and 2 (later, 3) EO tutors. Since roughly the same time initial desk training has been given to newcomers to pension work on special sections set up for training purposes within the divisions, while the needs of the novice computer programmer are now satisfied by five months' apprenticeship under the training officer in CB. The central training section now arranges a wide variety of external courses, including day-release for school leavers, specialist training at the Civil Service College and pre-retirement sessions at the Crawley College of Further Education.

Since 1972 one of the departmental tutors has doubled as the Office's part-time welfare officer, a post which was created when dispersal made it difficult for the Treasury welfare officer to serve the PGO from her London base. Among other welfare duties the PGO officer has overall responsibility for facilities and instructions in first aid. Fortunately a dedicated band of volunteers has been available for the first aid rota ever since it was set up at Crawley in 1966, and there has been no shortage of skilled instructors with previous experience, to arrange regular training and examinations.

Refreshment

Dispersal was the event which also triggered an improvement in the department's refreshment service. The history of luncheon facilities at the PGO began in 1867, when one of its own employees, Mr Reid, was assigned the task of preparing meals in a top floor room of the Whitehall office, in order to dissuade staff from leaving the building during office hours to lunch at the Treasury. In 1883 the 'purveyor' was granted £20 a year for his services to the inner man. Meal orders were collected each morning, accounts were rendered weekly to the customers, and there was no trolley service — staff had to make their own tea, using a gas-jet in the basement. As we have seen aready, the Whitehall club continued to give good service until the bombing of 1940. Around that time Mecca Cafes Ltd opened a cafeteria in the Dartmouth Street building, but many staff preferred to go to outside places of refreshment. At Somerset House the Inland Revenue canteen, too, was spurned by most PGO personnel, in favour of the more superior restaurant at Bush House (itself hit by a bomb), the government sponsored 'British restaurants' with their cheap prices but uncomfortable 'utility' furniture, and local cafes which served up soup and jacket potatoes until the gas was turned off at 3 pm. When the Office moved to Russell Square hopes of a rebirth of the PGO canteen were dashed, despite considerable efforts on the part of both staff and management, and the best that could be achieved was representation on the committee of the Ministry of Transport and Civil Aviation canteen in Woburn Place, which many staff used. Tea was now brewed by electric kettles in the work rooms and electric urns in the corridors.

At Crawley, however, provision was made for a purpose-built restaurant and bar, for the first time in the Office's history. From the outset it was run by a committee, appointed jointly by the DWC, in order to offer the best possible service, and with generous help from Messrs Whitbread in the construction of the bar, the restaurant opened for business on 5 August 1968, under the enthusiastic leadership of Denis Dutton (chairman), Stan Douglas (secretary) and Mrs Cooper, the manageress. A fortnight earlier the PGO's first trolley service had started to roll. In its first 16 years the restaurant's sales have risen from £12,000 to £58,000 a year, while bar takings have increased from £2,000 to £26,000. About 22,000 main meals and 16,000 bar snacks are curently sold annually; in addition the restaurant makes special Christmas and celebration lunches, and provides bar facilities for many evening functions. Despite competition from without, the PGO restaurant continues to be managed by a PGO committee, although in 1985 it had to revise the tariff to fall in line with those operating in the restaurants of other government departments.

Women's rights

For the first 50 years of the PGO's existence the Victorian attitude that women were fit only for domestic service or factory labour kept the Office an all-

PGO LADIES in 1928 at the sports afternoon, Chiswick. Top: the skipping race. Bottom: Mrs Taylor's keep fit class entertains.
Photos: R C S Taylor's album.

male bastion except for housemaids and charwomen. In the 1890s female typists were first employed, experimentally, but although they apparently proved to be 'an efficient and economical form of labour' the Treasury in 1894 were still finding reasons why their use might be restricted to 100 in the entire service.

> *In some instances the Heads of Departments prefer boy typists. In some instances the copying is of a nature that must be left to men. In some instances it is difficult to find in existing official buildings the separate rooms which a female staff requires. My Lords, therefore, are dealing with a very limited class of persons engaged on work of a mechanical character.*

To ensure that the women typists remained limited in number, their Lordships ordered that pay on entry should be 16s. (80p) a week, rising to 25s. at the maximum; new entrants should be taken on between the ages of 18 and 30; applicants should be examined in writing, spelling and arithmetic, as well as in typing; and they would have to leave as soon as they married — after all, as the Treasury saw it, 'a woman, as wife and mother, cannot be expected to work for the State continuously and effectively.'

In the early years of the 20th century the cause of women's rights, and particularly their claim to vote, was being actively and often aggressively pursued by the suffragette movement, and at least once the PGO's Whitehall office came under attack from stone-throwing sympathisers. However, in 1914 the suffragettes called a truce in order to add their considerable energies to the nation's war effort, and the desperate shortage of men forced even the civil service, including the PGO, to recruit women clerks. It was a purely temporary expedient, of course, to plug the gaps until the men returned from the war. However, when the war ended many of the women had to stay on to deal with the increased work arising from the growing numbers of effective payments and war pensions. The newly-installed adding machines and the mundane tasks of filing papers and index cards were seen by the Office as ideal for female labour. By April 1920 the PGO was employing 62 temporary women clerks, of whom 13 were Grade II (CO) and 49 were Grade III (writing assistants).

After the war, a series of civil service examinations resulted in the establishment of 1 female CO and, by 1922, 40 writing assistants, but still women were not let loose on pension section duties. The filing section at Caxton House West was a strictly all-female preserve, out of bounds to male officers — for the prevention of internal fraud, so Office management maintained. If a pension CO needed a file, a couple of girls had to put on hats and coats to take it round the corner to Dartmouth Street. Later in the 1920s some favoured women were given three months trial on CO effective duties, but generally the sexual segregation continued till 1935, when women COs first appeared on pension sections. Unmarried girls began to be recruited to the PGO in the late 1930s, but there was still hostility to the employment of women at a time of great job shortage. Some male members of the PGO belonged to organisations dedicated to keeping them out, but by 1939 about 35 per cent of the staff were women. None, however, was of higher rank than CO. The Staff Side (which itself had no female member before 1936) voiced an opinion which they apparently shared with management. 'Although very young girls were all right for routine duties', they said, 'older men were more suitable for the non-effective duties where greater experience of business life was required'.

During the 1939-45 war increasing numbers of female COs were taken on. In

1941 women were appointed to the supervisory rank of higher clerical officer (HCO) and at last, in 1943, Marie Nowell became the first woman EO in the PGO. Yet still some of the Victorian attitudes prevailed. The ban on married women persisted until 1946, although because of the wartime staff shortage a woman could continue in an unestablished capacity after marriage; women were trained in first aid, rifle shooting and resistance to gas warfare, but they were not allowed to take a turn at fire-watching — apparently the Assistant Paymaster General feared that nightly mixed fire parties might not give their full attention to duty; finally, women did not get equal wages for doing the same jobs as their male counterparts, except at the bottom end of the scales. When eventually equal pay was agreed in principle at national level it was phased over a seven year period and did not come into full effect until 1961. Further milestones were passed in 1944 when HCO Dorothy Horton was promoted as the Office's first female HEO ('staff officer'), and in 1958 when Helen Bottrill became its first woman SEO head of division.

It was dispersal that finally tilted the balance in numbers between the sexes: today women are dominant not only in the typing pool, data preparations room and telephone switchboard but also in the grades of CA, CO, EO, messenger and paperkeeper. They are also well represented in the specialised areas of computer programmer, systems analyst, computer operator and divisional manager, and in the last 20 years the Office has served under two female Paymasters General, Judith Hart and Shirley Williams. A reversal of the Victorian prejudice against women in clerical jobs, the increasing desire and necessity for wives to seek paid occupation and the availability of work-sharing and part-time employment have all contributed to the present situation where 65 per cent of the PGO's staff are women.

Celebrities

Apart from the many staff who have earned distinction through promotion and honours by service to the department, the PGO has had its share of celebrities who have made a name in other fields.

ROY HALLIDAY came to the Office in 1939 as a 17 year old CO. During the blitz he played an active role in the Home Guard and fire-watching party, and in October 1940 he helped to dig out casualties and belongings from the wreckage of the Whitehall office. In 1941 he joined the Royal Navy as a naval air cadet and after distinguished war service in which he was mentioned in despatches and earned the DSC, he decided to resign from the Office to follow a career in the navy. Before he did so he married Polly Meech, a PGO clerk who had served in the Office throughout the war. Halliday travelled the world with the navy, serving as test pilot, squadron commander of minesweepers and destroyers and at times having direct command of 8,000 men. By 1973 he had earned appointment as Director of Naval Intelligence. He became *aide-de-camp* to HM the Queen in 1974, and the following year was promoted to rear admiral commanding British naval staff. By the time his naval career ended in 1981 he was vice admiral and Deputy Chief of Staff for Intelligence. Knighted in the same year, he then resumed a civil service career as Director General of Intelligence at the Ministry of Defence. As Sir Roy says, his progression in the civil service from CO in the PGO direct to Deputy Under Secretary of State at the MOD must be 'unusual, and probably unique'. Sir Roy Halliday retired from the service in 1984 and is now 'the happy recipient of two pensions from the PGO'

EDMUND HARWOOD entered the PGO in 1921, also as a CO, at the age of 23. Four years later he was promoted controversially, having been specially selected by Roland Wilkins to fill the new EO post of private secretary to the Assistant Paymaster General, and was expected also to perform secretarial duties for the Minister, as and when required. It was Harwood who did much research into the Office's early history at Wilkins' behest, but he had to wait for another 10 years before achieving HEO rank. Shortly before the war, Harwood was one of the many who responded to the call of expanding departments which offered better prospects. He moved, on loan, to the Ministry of Food, where in 1940 he was promoted to assistant secretary. Not surprisingly he decided to stay with that department, rising to deputy secretary rank in 1953. Edmund Harwood was knighted in 1956, and after retirement three years later was appointed a member of the Milk Marketing Board and Chairman of National Cold Stores (Management) Ltd. He died in 1964.

Among others who made good after leaving the Office were HAROLD WHITMORE (1939-49) who went on to become a university professor in Australia, and JAMES DOBSON (1948-66), currently the Accountant at the House of Commons. Others have achieved high positions in local government while serving in the Office, and some have earned sporting honours.

In the world of entertainment the PGO has one claim to fame who was outstanding in every sense. GLADYS MILLS came to the Office in 1952 as a temporary typist. Her manual dexterity and commanding personality earned her quick promotion to the new post of superintendent of typists in 1955, a post which she was to hold for the next seven years. A large, jolly person with an infectious laugh 'Glad', as she liked to be called, was a gifted pianist, who after working hours entertained with her small group at public houses and parties around her Essex home. Once a year she would provide the accompaniment at the Office dinner and dance where her sparkling treatment of popular tunes was guaranteed to get the party going. Such was her reputation for playing by ear that at one such function dancers were surprised to see that she was apparently sight-reading, but the mystery was solved when Glad revealed that it was the Evening Standard she was reading as she played. The story goes that her fame reached the ears of a professional agent who sent a talent scout to one of Glad's engagements and without delay offered her a recording contract, followed by regular appearances on the Billy Cotton TV show.

At first Mrs Mills refused to turn her back on the security of her job in the PGO typing pool, and at lunchtimes she would go out to do her shopping, cut a record or two and return to Russell Square. Eventually, in 1962, she had to resign in order to fulfil the engagements which were now pouring in, and took her leave in a memorable farewell party attended by popular entertainer Frankie Vaughan. At the height of her popularity the Office was represented in a TV broadcast of 'This is Your Life, Mrs Mills' and was mentioned on the jacket of several of her records. Sadly, Glad's health declined after loss of her mother and her husband, and she was forced to retire from the entertainment business. She died in 1978, at the age of 60. However, like so many of those who have left the Office for pastures new, Gladys Mills never forgot her old department, and visited the new Crawley building soon after dispersal, to renew acquaintances. It's that sort of Office.

14. PLAYMASTERS : *the recreational side*

Pre-war origins

For such a small department, or perhaps because it is small and compact, the PGO has seen a remarkable variety of social and sporting activities, most of which are still enjoyed today. Unfortunately we have no evidence of what the Victorians or Edwardians got up to after office hours, but whatever it was it probably had nothing to do with the Office, for there are few surviving records of sports at the PGO before 1925. By that time the Office had about 300 staff, most of whom were young, active people of both sexes who had joined the PGO around the time of its post-war reorganisation. The time was right for the organisation of physical recreation, to provide some relief from the tedium of routine clerical and mechanical duties. Although no doubt some sports and games (golf, table tennis, cricket and chess, for example) had been in progress already in an informal way the real stimulus was provided when in 1925 the Duke of Sutherland decided to mark his appointment as Paymaster General by presenting a silver trophy, to be awarded for sporting competition in the PGO.

A committee, set up to adminster this SUTHERLAND CUP, agreed that it should be contested annually between the main (Whitehall) and branch (Dartmouth Street) offices, the trophy going to the office with the most victories in a series of nine events — association football, golf, cricket, tennis, rifle shooting, swimming, table tennis, billiards and chess. Pleased with the success of the first year's competition, his Grace generously donated a second, LADIES CUP, to be awarded solely for women's events. Since then, the two trophies have been competed for each year except for breaks during the war and the dispersal exercise. The component events have altered over the years, and so has the division of the Office into teams. The Ladies Cup survived only one year as main v branch office, and then changed to Orange v Green (from 1927 to 1954 the colours were allotted to girls on their first day in the department). In the Sutherland Cup, main office played branch office until the war, but with everyone in the same building at Russell Square the events were fought between Odds and Evens, allegiance being decided by the division (1D, 2D etc) in which one worked. In 1954 the ladies realigned as Alpha and Omega, according to their surnames, which method was adopted also for the Sutherland Cup in 1968. However, in 1982 the organisers wisely agreed that divisional loyalties were stronger than allegiance to a half of the alphabet and now, although the events are organised as Alpha v Omega, points are awarded for taking part and for being on the winning side, to enable the Sutherland Cup to be won by the division with the most successful competitors. The Ladies Cup is now awarded to the individual woman gaining the most points, and a new trophy, presented by Eric Webster on his retirement as Assistant Paymaster General, goes to the leading man.

One spin-off from the Sutherland Cup was the emergence from the original committee of a PGO SPORTS ASSOCIATION. Founded by John McIntyre and Dai Davies in 1931, and affiliated to the Civil Service Sports Council (CSSC), this initially comprised the golf and horticultural societies, the chess, swimming, table tennis and rifle clubs, and cricket and football sections. The Sports Association has looked after the department's sporting interests ever since, apart from a wartime break to 1948, when it was reactivated by Dai Davies and David Wheble. It receives income from the CSSC equivalent to the contributions made by Office members to their funds, and uses this to award grants or interest-free loans to new and existing clubs, assist with fees and expenses for teams and individuals entering CSSC competitions, and bear the cost of Sutherland Cup events. In 1953 it arranged the supply of PGO blazer badges and shirt crests to its members, but unfortunately this practice has now ceased. The Association also liaises with the CSSC over service-wide events, and awards annually the WHEBLE CUP to the Office's most promising youngster and the NORFOLK CUP to the leading club administrator. Its long-term dream is to own and manage a sports ground and clubhouse for PGO sportspeople.

A highlight of the social calendar while the Office was in London was the annual DINNER AND DANCE, at which the sports cups were usually presented. These rather formal functions took place in various hotels and restaurants in the west end and were usually attended by the Paymaster General, a large proportion of the staff and some of their retired colleagues. Tickets for the first dinner in 1926 cost just four shillings each, and 128 people were present. The programme for the 1938 event reveals that in addition to toasts and presentations there were songs by an Office baritone and a ladies' glee club, a professional comedy act and 'music by Nat Harris and his Broadcasting Quartet from the Bohemian Dance Club'. Tickets had risen to 6s. 6d, but the under 21s were allowed a reduction. By the early 1980s the formal dinner and dance had vanished from the social scene, through rising costs and the emergence of a new generation in Crawley, less inclined towards formality. The sports cups are now presented at an annual buffet dance arranged by the PGO Sports Association.

In 1927 the Sutherland Cup committee organised the first of half a dozen annual SPORTS AFTERNOONS at the civil service sports ground, Chiswick. Although serious athletic contests were included (including tug of war and relay races earning points for the Sutherland Cup), the programmes, photographs and personal memories of these occasions suggest that the afternoons were mainly fun occasions, when a traditionally staid and sober Office could let its hair down for a few hours in the year to take part in a degree of social contact and absurd activities which at any other time would have been thought quite shocking. As females were apparently considered incapable of serious athletic pursuit it was they who were involved in the more outrageous events — not just the inevitable egg and spoon and three-legged races but also skipping, walking on flower pots, running blindfold and making farmyard noises for the menfolk to guess. Their practice sessions in St James's Park and Horse Guards Parade must have raised many a Whitehall eyebrow. In front of a crowded spectator stand at Chiswick a military band accompanied the musical chairs, open air dancing and energetic displays by the keep fit class, trained by the Office's Mrs Taylor after working hours in a school near Victoria. Even the austere Mr Wilkins entered into the spirit of the occasion of this annual safety valve, as he donned an immaculate

SPORTS AFTERNOON at Crawley Leisure Centre, 1968. Top: Computer Branch supporters with their Panda mascot.
Reproduced by permission of Crawley News.
Bottom: finish of the 100 yard sprint.
Photo: Alan Lawrence.

light grey suit with matching trilby and white carnation to adjudicate the events and present the prizes.

By 1933 advancing years and the dearth of young recruits had caused the demise of the sports afternoon. An attempt to revive it at Russell Square failed through lack of support, but at Crawley the PGO ATHLETICS CLUB staged a sports afternoon annually between 1968 and 1978, in the conveniently placed arena just across the square from Sutherland House. Former colleagues were invited for lunch and to attend the sports, and in the evening the staff restaurant was the venue for a presentation dance. There are hopes that the Office's 150th year will see a new awakening of the annual sports. Certainly at Crawley there is a growing interest in lunchtime jogging.

Of the sporting and social activities pursued at the PGO before the war nearly all emerged apparently unscathed once the Office was reunited at Russell Square House. It is a strange fact that the war had less impact on these early pastimes than did dispersal to Crawley. Some of the activities did not make the move at all, but they were counterbalanced by others which have gone from strength to strength at their new home.

In the 1920s bridge, chess and billiards were well patronised by the Office hierarchy; some clerks who were skilful enough believed that participation might actually increase their slim chances of promotion. BILLIARDS continued to be a Sutherland Cup event until the 1950s, but has not re-emerged at Crawley. A BRIDGE club did reappear briefly not long after dispersal, but unfortunately was short lived. CHESS, however, has been a popular pastime continuously for at least 75 years. The chess club was certainly in existence in 1910, when a strong team competed in division 2 of the Civil Service and Municipal League, winning the handsome championship shield three times between 1911 and 1939. Top board for most of the time was James Mahood and second board R C S Taylor, both destined to become Assistant Paymasters General. Mahood did not relinquish the No 1 position until 1950, long after his retirement, when Taylor at last had his chance to take top board. When war stopped play in 1939 the team was still in division 2 and the club was meeting regularly for friendly and Sutherland Cup competitions. After the war, activity resumed in 1946, and by the end of the 1950s the club was fielding three league teams. A new trophy presented later, in memory of Mr Taylor, was awarded annually to the winner of a knockout competition. However, as the stronger players departed, relegation came to the PGO, and just before dispersal the club had been reduced to two league teams, playing in divisions 5 and 6. After a further two year break, players regrouped in Crawley, entered two teams in the new Mid Sussex Chess League with some success, and once more held club nights at the PGO, no doubt benefiting from the revival of interest in chess at the time of the Fisher v Spasky world championship match of 1970. Sadly in 1984 the chess club was unable to attract sufficient support, and its activities ceased. There are still many enthusiasts in the Office, and it must be only a matter of time before the club rises from the ashes for a fourth time.

CRICKET is another game which has been practised at the PGO since at least 1909, although there are no surviving records of its pre-war history apart from early photographs of matches against other clubs and references to Sutherland Cup matches at Catford. After the war the enthusiasm of Reg Grimer was instrumental in the reformation of the cricket club in 1952, the members being divided into active (the players) and passive ('those who cannot

PGO CRICKET in 1911: standing 6th from left is R C S Taylor and also standing, 3rd from right is James Mahood, both later Assistant Paymasters General.
Photo: R C S Taylor's album.

play but are willing to help the club financially by swelling the membership'). The sum of £35 necessary to buy new bats, balls, stumps, pads and other equipment was quickly raised by a grant from the Sports Association and membership subscriptions, and soon friendly matches were played on Saturday afternoons and weekday evenings at Eltham against a variety of teams, usually from other government departments. In the ensuing years the club built up strong support and ended its season with a 'flannel dance' at the Whitehall Gardens restaurant. Life at Crawley began promisingly with competitive games between the temporary PGO offices, and blossomed with the club's entry in the new Crawley Evening Cricket League, which it won in 1969. Regular weekend cricket also was played against local teams. The PGO has enjoyed little success in the service-wide Curtis-Bennett Shield, in which it is one of the smallest competing departments, but between 1969 and 1977 it won the CSSC regional three-a-side competition no less than four times. Regrettably interest has waned in recent years as the Office's cricketing talent has opted for the superior facilities of private clubs, and only intermittent games are now played.

Surprisingly the pre-dispersal interest in SWIMMING has not inspired the formation of a PGO club in Crawley, despite the existence of a pool at the nearby leisure centre. Nevertheless, many of the staff do make private use of the facilities both at lunchtime and after work. Swimming was certainly a popular activity between the wars, and in the 1950s staff patronised the YWCA baths in Great Russell Street in the lunch hour. Driven on by the enthusiasm of Harry Oxley, they competed in a civil service league, the Sutherland and Ladies Cups, and galas at various baths, including the staff pool at the Bourne and Hollingsworth department store.

TENNIS also was being played at the time of the first Sutherland Cup competition in 1925. In the 1930s players would brave the odours from a nearby sauce factory and brewery to enjoy twice-weekly club nights at Vauxhall, while ladies finals day was one of the highlights of the social calendar. It was held in the private tennis court at the Banstead home of one of the Office principals, Henry Botting. In those days of sexual inequality no men were invited, but all ladies who had taken part in the earlier rounds of the knockout cup were invited to attend and partake of the tea and homemade ice cream served by Mrs Botting and her daughter. By 1939 club evenings had moved to Archbishops Park, near Waterloo, where further factory smells had to be endured. After the war the tennis club was reformed in 1950 with the aid of a Sports Association grant of £5 and a donation of a guinea from the Assistant Paymaster General. A search for available courts led finally to Paddington recreation ground, where weekly club nights were held until 1966. Sutherland and Ladies Cup contests took place at Chiswick. After the trauma of dispersal the tennis club finally managed to evade unpleasant smells by settling at the Southgate recreation ground, where unfortunately playing numbers are restricted because only two courts are available. Through the good offices of a PGO contact, Sutherland Cup matches are now played annually at the Horley Lawn Tennis Club: these, together with weekly club nights and occasional social gatherings are the evidence that tennis continues to flourish in the PGO.

Another pastime which early photographs indicate was enjoyed mainly by the Office elite was GOLF. A golf society was one of the original affiliates to the PGO Sports Association, and held twice-yearly tournaments. At Russell Square there was an annual competition for a trophy presented by Assistant Paymaster General R C S Taylor, as well as golf's contribution to the Sutherland Cup. After dispersal, the society was re-established, holding monthly tournaments throughout the summer and ending with a whole-day contest at the Ifield Club, followed by an evening meal and presentation of trophies. The Office society participated in the Crawley Industrial League, becoming champions in 1976. At this time there were more than 30 members, but numbers later declined in the face of increasing costs and the society was obliged to withdraw from the league. Golfing activities, however, still take place annually in the shape of the Sutherland Cup match and a springtime challenge by the ever hopeful Young-uns against the experienced Old-uns. Hopefully the Taylor Trophy will once again be awarded to the Office's best golfer before too long.

Between the wars TABLE TENNIS was popular at the branch office in lunch breaks and after working hours. Contests took place for the Sutherland and Ladies Cups, and against other teams in friendly matches. After the wartime break the club was reformed in 1948, just after the first PGO staff moved into Russell Square House. In the basement there, amid the dusty files and under the puzzled stare of the occasional rat, matches were played in the London Civil Service League by up to four Office teams. League matches continued until 1966, and from 1958 club members were permitted to practice at lunchtimes, too. At Crawley, table tennis flourished as never before, at first in temporary accommodation and later in the reception room at Sutherland House (apart from two years when pressure of space forced the club to use huts elsewhere). Since 1965 the club has entered up to eight teams in the Crawley League

PGO SOCCER in 1930: the branch office team for the Sutherland Cup.
Photo: R C S Taylor's album.

winning several divisional titles and knockout competitions, and in 1974 gained 3rd place in the 1st division, its best performance yet. Between 1972 and 1978 PGO teams also won the CSSC regional competition three times. Internal Office tournaments have been well supported; the 1974 event attracted no fewer than 200 entries. In 1973 the club established a link with Le Havre Athletic Club table tennis section. For six years weekend exchange visits took place annually, each club playing host in alternate years and arranging sightseeing trips, dances and, of course, Anglo-French table tennis competitions. The PGO club has been fortunate in having members who show enthusiasm and commitment as well as skill, and special credit in all of these respects goes to Eric Webster, the post-war driving force in PGO table tennis and later a player-pensioner.

Before the war a PGO RIFLE SHOOTING club used a range at the War Office and took part in a league competition for the Vickers Bowl. Its post-war revival had to wait until 1976, when members were able to shoot at a purpose-built gallery at Crawley leisure centre in the lunch hour. This range was later converted to other uses, and the club moved on to the Territorial Army drill hall (once used by the PGO as a temporary office). The club was eventually wound up in 1981, when under the flexible working hours scheme staff began to opt for shorter lunch breaks.

There was no ASSOCIATION FOOTBALL club in the 1920s, but occasional friendly matches and the annual Sutherland Cup fixture took place. In the 1930s even these proved impossible because of the scarcity of young men, and the few youngsters who did desire a regular game had to join teams run by other departments. In 1950, around a table as they sorted weekly pension foils, a PGO football club was at last formed by Don Donovan, Albert Wood and the ubiquitous Reg Grimer. They were refused permission for members to take a regular half-day's leave in order to play in a midweek league, so in 1951 entered a team in the London Civil Service League, under the captaincy of former Northern Ireland schoolboy international Alf McClatchey. Home matches were played at Parliament Hill Fields, Chiswick and Eltham, while away games took the team to romantic destinations such as Watford, Wormwood Scrubs and the Hackney marshes. There were no major achievements during this period, but one creditable performance in narrowly losing in the semi-finals of the London Civil Service six-a-side competition. Participation in the London league ended in 1964, but within two years the club was reborn in Crawley, and the team was promoted in its first season in the Crawley and District League. In the 1970s the club entered three teams in the league, won the CSSC regional indoor five-a-side tournament in 1979, finished runner-up in division 1 in 1977/8 and appeared in two cup finals, for the Mid Sussex Junior Charity Cup in 1969/70 and the Crawley Senior Cup in 1977/8. In the 1971 Reg Brown independently founded a 'Panda Juniors' team for the sons of Office members. This, too, earned honours in a local (under 12s) league, and several years later the original lads emerged as a major force in the Crawley League. Among the PGO football club's highlights have been exchange visits with two clubs from Dorsten, Crawley's twin town close to the Ruhr area of West Germany. Between 1979 and 1984 there were three trips in each direction to enjoy hospitality, see the sights and play soccer. Now once again reduced to one team and renamed 'Paymasters', the football club has built up a proud reputation for sportsmanship on the field, its members have earned representative honours for the Crawley League and its officials have taken a leading role in league affairs. The club's longest serving active member, Barry Bartholomew (with nearly 30 years' service to PGO football) is currently the league's treasurer.

BOWLS was the game which in the 1930s replaced football as a Sutherland Cup event, but there is no evidence that a club existed in the PGO or of any activity after the war. On the other hand, HOCKEY was a Ladies Cup event before the war, and in 1936 was being run by a formally constituted club. It has since been resurrected on a less formal basis at both Russell Square and Crawley. On one occasion in 1939 the men were bold enough to challenge the ladies, and ran out 6-0 winners despite claiming ignorance of the rules. After dispersal, attempts were made to raise a team to play regular fixtures, but only friendly and CSSC matches have been played so far, and a set of hockey sticks remains in store for the next revival.

Another pastime enjoyed by the ladies of the PGO before the war was NETBALL, which was played in the school where Mrs Taylor conducted her keep fit course. Internal games continued after the war, and by 1952 a club had been formed, to play matches in a civil service league at Lincolns Inn Fields. Since 1975 the club has entered two teams in the Crawley Netball League, playing its home games in the Office car park. Several of its members have earned sporting honours in the Office and two have been selected to play for the Crawley netball team. The club owes much to the reliable Peter Snell, its regular, all-weather umpire since Russell Square days.

Between the wars many non-sporting recreational pursuits were being organised. PGO clerks of those days recall the social excursions which were arranged after work and at weekends, among them visits to the postal sorting office at Mount Pleasant, the Daily Mirror headquarters, Vauxhall brewery and even the top of Big Ben. Once there was a tour of Limehouse which included the rare chance of a meal in a Chinese restaurant, while one Saturday a rambling enthusiast led an unsuspecting party through 25 miles of the Surrey countryside and up the steep side of Box Hill. At Russell Square House the Civil Service Clerical Association arranged visits to the circus, dances in local hotels to supplement the annual Sports Association event, and in 1951 a river trip to Kew, returning after dark to see the Festival of Britain illuminations. Theatre clubs operated independently within the the divisions to provide the occasional night out for weekly contributors. However, it was after dispersal that the organisation of social events was put on a formal footing.

The PGO SOCIAL CLUB was founded towards the end of 1968 under the leadership of Gerry McDowell (chairman), Bill Wing (secretary), John Southall (treasurer) and Jeff Gayler as chief organiser. In the early days theatre trips to London, dances in the staff restaurant and car rallies through the countryside were the main events on offer. During the early 1970s Sid Perry produced the first Music Hall night, then staged on four table tops precariously resting on a collection of beer barrels. This disclosed a wealth of musical talent which was soon to lead to two or three performances of each show. The following year saw the birth of Singalong' evenings which have continued to exercise PGO tonsils to the present day. There were also downland rambles, arts and crafts shows and, in 1975, the first visit to foreign parts, a weekend at the Belgian beer festival. This aspect of the club's activities has taken off in more ways than one, for in the last eight years there have been excursions to Paris, Rome, the Dutch bulbfields, Switzerland, Andalucia, Athens, Istanbul and on two occasions the Soviet Union. The visit to Athens attracted no less than 90 staff and their friends. Theatre trips have now extended to nights at the opera and ballet, to see classics such as Cavalleria Rusticana, The Marriage of Figaro and Swan Lake, and to the modern-day musicals Evita, Annie, Cats and many others. The social club has indeed widened its horizons since the early days. The annual turnover has increased from less than £500 in 1969 to £26,000 in 1984, a success story which is due to the vision of a small band of founder members and immeasurably to the industrious Janet Williams, the club's secretary since 1976. A healthy bank balance, a varied and interesting programme and the continuing support of the PGO staff should ensure the prosperity of the social club for many years to come.

For the staff who wished to channel their efforts into service for others a SOCIAL SERVICE association was formed in 1936 but apparently did not survive the war. However, at Crawley in the late 1960s several Office members volunteered to assist the FLAMINGOES SWIMMING CLUB, by providing transport and help in the pool for physically disabled people, under a scheme supported by the local council. Some staff still take part in the weekly transport rota, in 1985.

One of the PGO's major successes, the HORTICULTURAL SOCIETY was formed at a meeting on 25 October 1929 to provide facilities for members to exchange plants and cuttings, purchase plants and sundries at discount rates, hold annual shows, arrange outings and provide an advisory service to members. Oddly enough one of the outings planned at the inaugural meeting was a visit to Cheal's Nurseries at Crawley. From the outset the society was supported by Roland Wilkins, who accepted the post of president and presented

HORTICULTURAL TRADING STORE at Sutherland House.
Photo: Ken Bridle, 1985.

for show competition an ornate trophy in memory of his wife. However, this did not prevent Mr Wilkins from taking chairman Reginald Wiltshier to task for using official stationery, franked envelopes and typing services for society correspondence, and for unwisely having Wilkins's name printed on notepaper used for conducting external business. Activities came to a halt in 1939, but were resumed in 1948 and have continued without a break until the present day, thanks to many dedicated people — in particular John Bell, Sid Gardner and Doris Hillier, who gave long service as chairman, secretary and treasurer respectively. In 1948 a small trading store was opened in a brick built warden's shelter in the well area of Russell Square House, and when this proved to be too wet it was moved to the basement of the main building. After the move to Crawley the store soon reappeared in the Old Post Office, and at Sutherland House it has had three different locations. It is the success of the trading store (sales of £277 in 1949 had risen to £11,700 by 1983) which is largely responsible for the society's low subscription rate and high membership. The original subscription of two shillings (10p) in 1929 was still the rate in 1977, and even now is only 20p a year, a bargain which is surely appreciated by today's 750 members.

Between one and three flower shows a year have been held throughout the society's existence. Again the invaluable basement was the venue in Russell Square House, while in the early days at Crawley the entrance hall of Goffs Park House and the West Green community centre were used. Since the opening of Sutherland House use has been made of the recreation room. Classes include flowers, fruit, vegetables, cookery and floral art; in addition to the Wilkins trophy there is now competition for cups presented by former Assistant Paymasters General John Vetch and Freddie Clay, the wife of R C S Taylor and the family of popular SEO Mary Pollard, in her memory. There is also a silver salver for cookery classes, donated by the society's committee. The judges have always been provided by the Guild of Civil Service Show Judges, a still active section of the now defunct Civil Service Horticultural Federation. In the pre-war years Mr Wiltshier issued monthly gardening notes based on his own knowledge and experience. This service was resumed from 1958 until today by John Bell's articles in the Office house magazine, TAG; during years when TAG was not published the society issued its own newsletters once more, under the title 'Greenfingers'. One further service given by the horticultural society has been the maintenance of flower arrangements beneath the Office war memorial since its unveiling in 1954.

Russell Square born

TAG was one of the institutions born at Russell Square House, first appearing in October 1950 under the editorship of Wally Hicks. Priced 3d (1p) a copy, it consisted of about 10 small, white, duplicated sheets, tagged or stapled together and containing contributions from PGO staff on topics ranging from sport to union activities, with poems, letters to the editor and articles of general interest such as the history of the Bloomsbury area. Although compiled by volunteers, TAG has been published monthly ever since, apart from brief interruptions after which it has always re-emerged, stronger than ever under new management. Now 6p a copy it is twice the size, with coloured pages and printing by offset litho, which allows better reproduction of the illustrations. A glance through the letters in back numbers of TAG is a walk through the Office's social history over the last 35 years, for here one finds pointed and sometimes cynical comment on controversial issues such as draughty offices, crowded rooms, social apathy, promotion policy and inter-divisional rivalry. Today's TAG comprises a mixture much as before, with articles on hobbies, sports and social events, ideas for holidays or eating places, horticultural and cookery hints, countryside topics, quizzes and crossword puzzles. With sales of nearly 600 the magazine clearly continues to fill a need within the Office.

Among TAG's regular features have been contributions by the PGO CHRISTIAN FELLOWSHIP. It was in 1950 that the Establishment Officer of the day sanctioned the formation of a branch of the Civil Service Christian Union and granted permission for its members to hold weekly lunchtime meetings in a room at Russell Square House, subject to a strict ban on all hymn singing. Once a year this restriction was lifted, to allow a carol service complete with accompaniment from a borrowed harmonium to be held in the all-purpose basement. Weekly meetings have continued to be the focus of activities, apart from the inevitable break caused by the disruption of dispersal. The branch was reformed in 1968 with the new title of PGO Christian Fellowship. Today its Tuesday lunchtime meetings provide an opportunity for Christians to join together for prayer and Bible study, to share in the work of Christian missions and to witness to the good news of salvation. Since moving to Crawley a local church has been used as a venue for the annual carol service which is now an established event in the PGO calendar.

Shortly after the birth of the Christian Union branch came the first meeting of a new DISCUSSION GROUP in 1951, but it seems that this was short lived and no similar activity has yet been started in Crawley. However, one activity which has been reborn in the New Town is MOUNTAINEERING. In Russell Square days and shortly after dispersal Mike West led excursions to the more rugged areas of Britain and to the sandstone rocks of northern Sussex. Recently enthusiasm was revived when the same leader and the same trusty rope were accompanied by a small PGO party to Snowdonia in April 1983. By the end of the year a Panda Mountaineering Club had been formed and a further visit arranged. In 1984, increasingly popular and successful walking and climbing trips were made to the same region, interspersed by speciality climbs in Wales, Purbeck, the Peak District and Glencoe, which provide harder and more varied routes than southern sandstone can offer. Snow and ice climbing are the latest venture of this club, the newest to be affiliated to the PGO Sports Association.

Crawley crop

The facilities available in the Crawley area and within the new PGO building have inspired a crop of activities which had not appeared previously within the Office. It was the prospect of peaceful, rhododendron bordered lakes at Ifield, Tilgate and Milton Mount and the promise of friendly competition on the banks of the lazy, winding rivers of Sussex that prompted the formation of a COARSE ANGLING club only a few months before the arrival of the first advance party in Crawley. In the experienced hands of secretary/organiser Jeff Gayler, the new club began to arrange informal meets and Sutherland Cup fixtures. Between 1982 and 1984 a team of its members, under the name Redfins, three times emerged as a qualifier for CSSC national finals, following success in consecutive regional competitions fished on the river Rother; unfortunately the PGO team were somewhat overshadowed in the wet of Windsor, the Lincolnshire frost and the blustery winds of Bath by opposition which took itself a trifle too seriously. In the PGO, angling remains a pastime of mental relaxation, far removed from the cares of official duties.

TENPIN BOWLING first made an impact on the PGO in 1966, when the CS pension divisions found themselves in Sussex House, next door to the newly-built Crawley bowling alley. Soon bowling became a regular lunchtime activity, and a mixed doubles league was started by Trevor Crowhurst. By 1969 this and two lunchtime leagues for four-person teams were in operation, but during the 1970s a single weekly league emerged, with promotion and relegation between the two divisions and trophies for the champions of each. In 1982 a knock out competition was first organised for the summer months. During the past two years an upsurge in interest has led to the two divisions having to bowl on different days, because the number of teams is greater than the Bowl's capacity. More than 100 people now take part each week. In 1983 a PGO bowling club was formally constituted and affiliated to the Sports Association. It now runs the competitions, maintains a prize fund for individual performances and enters teams in tournaments organised by the Civil Service Ten Pin Bowling Association and the Crawley Bowl. Office members have enjoyed considerable success in such competitions, reaching the national finals of the first CSSC championships in 1984 and of the Courage championships three times, once finishing as runners-up. Bowling is an activity which continues to thrive despite the pressures of flexible working hours and the increasing cost of participation. Its success owes much to the secretarial work of John Fraser, who has been organising the leagues since 1969 and still manages to be one of the best bowlers.

At Crawley, a PHILATELIC club operated for a few years just after the dispersal, STOOLBALL and ROUNDERS also have been organised formally for brief periods but now continue only intermittently in nearby playing fields. Adherents of SQUASH and BADMINTON have excellent facilities at the leisure centre, and both have been popular lunchtime activities since that centre opened soon after dispersal. A squash club was formed in the 1970s, but its members have preferred to play informally arranged matches rather than league or cup games. Squash and badminton are both now Sutherland Cup events, and in 1984 a badminton club was formed which runs singles and doubles leagues. In the 1980s a HORSE RIDING club was in existence briefly. RUGBY FOOTBALL has never been put on a formal basis in the PGO, but occasionally it makes an appearance as a Sutherland Cup event.

The staff restaurant and bar facilities of Sutherland House were quickly recognised as potentially suitable for events such as parties and dances, and divisional CHRISTMAS PARTIES have been held there for the past 17 years. In the 1970s attempts were made to form a DRAMA group, but had to be shelved when leading players were sent away on training courses. In October 1968 Dave Skam arranged a meeting to assess interest in a club for enthusiasts of BALLROOM and LATIN AMERICAN DANCING. More than 30 people attended, a club was formed on the spot and continued to operate for seven years under the tutorship of Dave and his wife, Doreen. Dances were held twice yearly, sometimes attracting 140 dancers and always boosting bar sales. At the end of 1975 activities came to an end as a result of retirements and resignations from the Office and a general change in musical tastes. The HAPPY DAZE DISCOTHEQUE, run by John Moon, gave pleasure and fun to the younger element for 10 years from 1971. Today the staff restaurant is the scene of an annual REUNION FOR PENSIONERS of the PGO. This began in 1981, following the cessation of sports afternoons to which retired colleagues were formerly invited. For the past four years more than 100 have attended the reunion to meet old friends and enjoy a meal and the hospitality of the Office's current staff. The first reunion was marked by an exhibition of Office history and the first three were also entertained by members of the Social Club's music hall artistes.

DARTS is a pastime which also is based in the bar area and which has grown in strength constantly since its formation in 1970. Originally organised by Stan Murray-Zmijewski (chairman) and the office services trio of John Hannam, Fred Feline and Fred Mills, at first it entered one team in the Crawley and District Darts League. Today the PGO has three men's and three ladies' teams in the league, and although to date they have no major achievements the club remains strongly supported by one of the largest memberships of any affiliate to the Sports Association. David Wheble, the club's first president, donated the President's Trophy, the most sought after of all internal competition cups, and the club arranges annual Sutherland Cup and inter-divisional darts competitions.

The past year has seen the formation of two new societies, whose programmes are only just beginning to take shape. Towards the end of 1984 a CAMERA club was formed, to promote the study and practice of photography. Regular meetings are held, newsletters issued and magazines circulated, while the club also has a small library of technical books to loan to its members. Early in 1985 the club was commissioned to take portraits of senior managers and heads of divisions; these will be included in an Office 'family tree', to be displayed in the central training section. The HISTORY society, founded by Maureen Wicks, has the formidable task of catering for an extremely wide range of interests, from local history to genealogy and antiques to archaelogy. Following an inaugural meeting in March 1985 it has heard speakers on Old Crawley and family history, and proposes to arrange visits to stately homes and other places of historical interest.

Currently the Office also has representatives of three trade unions and many other national organisations which provide a valuable service: the Civil and Public Services Association, Civil Service Union, Society of Civil and Public Servants, Civil Service Benevolent Fund, Civil Service Lifeboat Fund, Civil Service Motoring Association, Hospital Saving Association, Hospital Saturday Fund, London Area Mobile Physiotherapy Service, Post Office and Civil Service Sanatorium Society and Post Office Insurance Society.

In such a brief summary of PGO leisure activities it is impossible to name all who have played important roles in each sport or pastime, and mention has been confined to only a few of the pioneers in each one. Nor has it been possible to make mention of the individual stars who have taken the limelight for a brief spell or over many years. Since dispersal so many achievements come to mind, including a 277 bowling score by Roger Spinks, Ken Bridle's 43 and Alf McClatchey's 33 goals in the football club's second league season, Trevor Crowhurst's completion of the London marathon course on two occasions, Alan Collyer's 102 for the cricket club and Sally Weston's appearance in the civil service national table tennis finals. With so many and so varied pastimes represented in the department it is perhaps surprising to find no mention of ARCHERY, BASKETBALL, CYCLING, MARTIAL ARTS, SNOOKER or WATER SPORTS. Perhaps this chapter may stimulate latent talent and generate interest in these, and other activities which once thrived in the PGO but now lie dormant.

15. FUTURE : *towards 2000*

To assess what may lie ahead for a department with 150 years of service already to its credit, I spoke to the present Assistant Paymaster General (Laurie Andrews), the head of the Pensions and Administration Branch (Dennis Breed), the head of Computer and Banking Services (Alf McClatchey), several of their predecessors and four of our post-war Ministers.

Without exception they were convinced that in the foreseeable future the PGO would remain a viable unit for making government payments and adminstering pensions. While some of the politicians wished to see further privatisation of public services where this would be more economical, even they doubted whether all or any of the PGO's functions could be performed more efficiently in other hands. It seems that the financial principles established by Burke in the 18th century; Parnell's visionary concept of a unified pay office; the sound, basic procedures which withstood the persistent attacks of Victorian antagonists; the bold decision to move from central London to the provinces; and the enormous technological advances of the last 30 years have all helped the Office to build up a universal reputation for reliability, service and efficiency. It is a reputation which speaks for itself by attracting more and more business each year. The PGO systems are now so complex and so inseparable, and its volume of transactions so vast, that to set up any of its functions elsewhere would not only be extremely costly but would also create unthinkable problems of staffing and training in order to achieve anything like the existing standards of service. Nevertheless, I found no trace of complacency. Both managers and Ministers hold the view that the Office must not simply maintain its present level of efficiency, but strive to increase it. Moreover, it must be able to demonstrate that it can perform its basic functions as government banker, provider of financial statistics and payer of pensions, more economically than any potential competitor. If it can do that, its future will be assured.

There is a firm belief at the PGO that there is very little scope for economising at the expense of the existing service to pensioners or customer departments. Therefore today the department's managers seek ways of making financial savings through improvement, rather than reduction, in the services now given. Thanks to the promise of advancing office technology there is every chance that this seemingly impossible dream can be realised.

Certainly the changes introduced in the last six years give rise to optimism. Bank lodgment details are now received on magnetic tape, which can be input direct to PANDA; the new pension system is able to perform many functions which previously had to be done manually; pension address records have all been postcoded; new sophisticated despatch equipment has been installed to enable vouchers, advices and P60s to go to the Post Office already sorted to postal districts and walks; P14 tax figures now go direct to the Inland Revenue on magnetic tape, rather than being printed; payments to pensioners' bank

PAYMASTER GENERAL JOHN GUMMER is shown a visual display unit in the central post opening room, during his visit in December 1984.
Photo: Ken Bridle.

accounts are put on a BACS tape, for credit by direct transfer; teachers' pensions are notified by magnetic tape, which is fed straight into the PGO computer; PANDA now holds a master index of all pensions, for on-line access by the post rooms; and details of weekly paid pension records can be called up instantly on visual display units. All this has happened within the space of six years. Each measure has both helped to reduce administration costs in the PGO, and contributed to a better service to the customer, in terms of speed, accuracy, reliability or a combination of all three.

So what more can be done? In the short term there are plans to extend the on-line interrogation system to embrace monthly and quarterly pensions, thus reducing the need for paper printouts and minimising delays in answering enquiries. Later the system could be developed to enable PANDA to accept changes to pension records via the visual display units on pension sections, to eliminate some of the form-filling and update the computer record as quickly as possible. More awarding departments are expected to pass pension details to the PGO on magnetic tape: direct input to the computer system will reduce clerical calculation and transcription and allow pension sections to take on more interesting and satisfying work.

The major advance in the long term is likely to be the development of electronic transfer — the transmission of data by telephone lines direct between computers. This will speed and simplify the sending of schedule details, interrogations, superannuation awards, income tax codes and GMP particulars to the PGO, and theP14s, statements of account, interrogation replies and lists of out-of-date issues from PANDA to the customer departments. This, too, will minimise clerical handling and the risk of transcription or keying errors. Some of the large departments may be able to provide this service sooner rather than later; the smaller issuing points may first take some intermediate step such as preparing schedules which can be optically read by computer peripheral machines at the PGO. Pension sections will be transformed not only by the presence of visual display terminals and a reduction in the volume of paper but also by the disappearance of space-consuming, room-darkening filing cupboards, when correspondence can be stored on computer media rather than pension files. Such developments are bound to be phased, because the limited resources of the Office would be unable to make everything happen at once, even if this were feasible. In practice, a gradual changeover to these new systems will enable both management and the Trade Union Side to assess the results stage by stage, and achieve any consequent economies without detriment to the serving staff or the service to customers.

Office management do not expect the department to be asked to take on additional, unrelated functions. What is likely, however, is that continued improvements in the department's cost-effectiveness will attract even more business of the type in which we specialise. Only recently the PGO system was found to be the most competitive for handling payments by the National Health Service Family Practitioner Committees, and the 400,000 transactions a year received from 99 issuing points could well be the start of further work for the NHS. The Office already administers 1,200,000 pensions, but there are still others in the public service, including many of the 'fringe' bodies, which the PGO does not handle, and these may well come our way in the course of time. To make use of the PGO's tried and tested computer systems and its expertise in pensions administration and government banking would seem both logical and cost-effective, even if it means some enhancement to the existing equipment.

Efficiency could be further improved by persuading more 'voucher' pensioners to accept payment direct to their bank accounts and encouraging those paid by the costly weekly method to be paid monthly. There is scope also for greater standardisation of public service pension schemes which would simplify procedures, reduce the different forms in use at the PGO, ease the training overheads and enable greater mobility of staff. This, however, must be a far-off dream because of the many hoops which such a move would have to pass through. It is ironic that this was one of Parnell's ambitions in 1841.

As far as accommodation is concerned the effects of new office technology such as the removal of filing cabinets should enable the PGO to fit within the present building for many years to come. None of those to whom I spoke wishes to see the Office grow too large, and the main hope is to keep its numbers below 1,000 for the foreseeable future. It will be no mean feat to restrict a department with so important a role and a steadily increasing workload to a size equivalent to about half that of the average comprehensive school.

The common threads running through most of my discussions while researching this book have been pride in past achievements, confidence in the future and satisfaction at being associated with an Office whose staff strive to give service to others. But above all pervades a view which no doubt would be shared to many in central government, that 'small is beautiful'. With 150 years on the board already, the PGO innings is by means closed.

16. MINISTERS :
Paymasters General 1836 - 1985

Year of appointment	
1836	Sir Henry Brooke PARNELL
1841	Edward John STANLEY
1841	Sir Edward KNATCHBULL
1845	William Bingham BARING
1846	Thomas Babington MACAULAY
1848	Earl GRANVILLE (Granville George LEVESON-GOWER)
1852	Baron STANLEY of ALDERLEY (Edward John STANLEY)
1852	Baron COLCHESTER (Charles Abbot)
1853	Baron STANLEY of ALDERLEY (Edward John STANLEY)
1855	Edward Pleydell BOUVERIE
1855	Robert LOWE
1858	Earl of DONOUGHMORE (Richard John HELY-HUTCHINSON)
1859	Baron LOVAINE of ALNWICK (Algernon George PERCY)
1859	James WILSON
1859	William Francis COWPER
1860	William HUTT
1865	George Joachim GOSCHEN
1866	William MONSELL
1866	Stephen CAVE
1868	Baron DUFFERIN AND CLANDEBOYE (Frederick Temple Hamilton BLACKWOOD)
1872	Hugh Culling Eardley CHILDERS
1873	William Patrick ADAM
1874	Stephen CAVE
1880	Hon David R PLUNKET
1880	Baron WOLVERTON (George Grenfell GLYN)
1885	Earl BEAUCHAMP (Frederick LYGON)
1886	Baron THURLOW (Thomas John Howell THURLOW-CUMMING-BRUCE)
1886	Earl BEAUCHAMP (Frederick LYGON)
1887	Earl BROWNLOW (Adelbert Wellington Brownlow CUST)
1889	Earl of JERSEY (Victor Albert George CHILD-VILLIERS)
1891	Baron WINDSOR (Robert George WINDSOR-CLIVE)
1892	Charles SEALE-HAYNE
1895	Earl of HOPETOUN (John Adrian Louis HOPE)
1899	Duke of MARLBOROUGH (Charles Richard John SPENCER-CHURCHILL)
1902	Sir Savile Brinton CROSSLEY

Year of appointment	
1906	Richard Knight CAUSTON
1910	Hon Ivor Churchill GUEST/Lord ASHBY ST LEDGERS
1912	Baron STRACHIE (Edward STRACHEY)
1915	Baron NEWTON (Thomas Wodehouse LEGH)
1916	Arthur HENDERSON
1916	Sir Joseph COMPTON-RICKETT
1919	Sir John Tudor WALTERS
1923	Arthur Neville CHAMBERLAIN
1923	Sir William JOYNSON-HICKS
1923	Major Archibald Boyd BOYD-CARPENTER
1924	Harry GOSLING
1925	Duke of SUTHERLAND (George Granville Sutherland EGERTON)
1928	Earl of ONSLOW (Richard William Alan ONSLOW)
1929	Baron ARNOLD (Sydney ARNOLD)
1931	Sir John Tudor WALTERS
1931	Baron ROCHESTER (Ernest Henry LAMB)
1935	Baron HUTCHISON of MONTROSE (Robert HUTCHINSON)
1938	Earl of MUNSTER (Geoffrey William Richard Hugh FITZ-CLARENCE)
1939	Earl WINTERTON (Edward TURNOUR)
1940	Viscount CRANBOURNE (Robert Arthur James GASCOYNE-CECIL)
1941	Baron HANKEY (Maurice Pascal Alers HANKEY)
1942	Sir William Allen JOWITT
1942	Baron CHERWELL (Frederick Alexander LINDEMANN)
1945	post vacant
1945	Arthur GREENWOOD
1947	Hilary Adair MARQUAND
1948	Viscount ADDISON (Christopher ADDISON)
1949	Baron MACDONALD of Gwaenysgor (Gordon MACDONALD)
1951	Baron CHERWELL (Frederick Alexander LINDEMANN)
1953	Earl of SELKIRK (George Nigel DOUGLAS-HAMILTON)
1955	post vacant
1956	Sir Walter Turner MONCKTON
1957	Reginald MAUDLING
1959	Viscount MILLS (Percy Herbert MILLS)
1961	Henry BROOKE
1962	John BOYD-CARPENTER
1964	George WIGG
1967	post vacant
1968	Baron SHACKLETON (Edward Arthur Alexander SHACKLETON)
1968	Judith HART
1969	Harold LEVER
1970	Viscount ECCLES (David McAdam ECCLES)

1973	Maurice MACMILLAN
1974	Edmund DELL
1976	Shirley WILLIAMS
1979	Angus Edward Upton MAUDE
1981	Francis Leslie PYM
1981	Cecil Edward PARKINSON
1983	post vacant
1984	John Selwyn GUMMER

17. APGs : *Assistant Paymasters General, 1836 - 1985*

Year of appointment	
1836	Terrick HAULTAIN
1841	William G ANDERSON
1854	Ernest A HOFFAY
1859	Morgan H FOSTER
1867	John P COLLIER
1885	post vacant
1892	Charles J MAUDE
1910	Charles Ll DAVIES
1924	Roland WILKINS
1935	James MAHOOD
1938	Leonard CUTHBERTSON
1945	Richard C S TAYLOR
1952	Alfred H MAY
1955	Cyril C WEST
1956	John H VETCH
1971	Frederick J CLAY
1978	Norman C NORFOLK
1980	Eric F WEBSTER
1982	Laurence A ANDREWS

SUTHERLAND HOUSE, built in 1966-8, and the extension built in 1975-6.
Photo: Ken Bridle, 1985.

18. MILESTONES :
notable dates in PGO history

1830	Consolidated pay office recommended by Sir Henry Parnell.
1835	Creation of the PGO authorised by Act of Parliament.
1836	Consolidation of the armed services pay offices: birth of the PGO.
1837	Closure of Dublin office.
1841	PGO takes over cash payment from Bank of England cashiers.
1845	PGO takes over work of Agent of Chelsea pensions.
1846	Greenwich out-pensions transferred to War Office: Tower Hill office closed.
1848	PGO takes over work of Paymasters of Exchequer Bills and Paymaster of Civil Services, including civil service pensions.
1856	Dockyard payments taken over by Admiralty: offices at Chatham, Sheerness, Plymouth and Portsmouth closed.
1857	Select Committee on Public Monies approves the PGO's handling of cash balances.
1861	PGO takes over work of Paymaster of Civil Services in Ireland and again has an office in Dublin.
1862	Closure of Hanover office.
1864	PGO takes over work of Office of Receiver of Constabulary in Ireland.
1866	Supply account opened at Bank of England.
1867	Monthly payment of salaries introduced. Luncheon club opened at PGO Whitehall office.
1869	Monthly payment of pensions begins. PGO ceases sending cashier to Chelsea Hospital.
1872	PGO takes over work of Accountant General of the Court of Chancery.
1878	Departments take over from PGO cashiers the payment of salaries in cash.
1885	W H Smith inquiry recommends abolition of PGO: Assistant Paymaster General post remains vacant for 7 years.
1889	Abolition of PGO authorised by Act of Parliament.
1890	PGO salaries vote merged with that of Treasury.
1894	Women typists first employed.
1896	Treasury decides not to abolish PGO. Working hours increased to 7 a day.
1898	Publication of Bartlett's Memorandum on the Business of the Office.
1899	PGO takes on payment of teachers' pensions.
1909	PGO takes on issue and payment of retirement lump sums.

1910-12	Refacing of west front of Whitehall office.
1914-18	Great War: loss of male clerks and increase of work leads to recruitment of women clerks.
1918	Serial numbering and standard size of payable orders introduced.
1919	English teachers' pensions transferred to Board of Education.
	Whitehall staff move into converted fodder store and temporary huts.
	Creation of Departmental Whitley Council.
1921	Montagu House Bungalows occupied.
1922	Creation of Irish Free State: Dublin office closed and RIC pensions transferred to PGO.
	Major reorganisation of the department.
1923	Branch office opened at Queen Anne's Gate Buildings, Dartmouth Street.
1925	Saturday afternoon closure introduced officially.
	Duke of Sutherland presents a cup for sports competitions.
1926	PGO takes back English teachers' pensions.
	Duke of Sutherland presents the 'Ladies Cup'.
	Office reorganised by divisions.
1927	First sports afternoon at Chiswick.
1928	Income tax assessment on salaries transferred to Inland Revenue.
1931	Income tax assessment on pensions transferred to Inland Revenue.
	Creation of PGO Sports Association.
1935	Women COs first employed on pension duties.
1937	Payment at sight introduced.
	War precautions begin.
1939	Weekly payment first made to civil service pensioners.
	Bank lodgment section moved to Stoke on Trent with bankers' clearing house.
1939-45	Second World War: further increases in payments and pensions.
1940	Whitehall office partially demolished by an enemy bomb: 3 PGO staff killed. Staff moved to Cornwall House and Somerset House.
1942	49 hour working week introduced.
1943	Promotion of first woman to EO.
1946	Lodgment section return from Stoke on Trent.
	End of marriage bar for women.
	26 Queen Anne's Gate and Queen Anne's Chambers occupied.
1947	First staff move to Russell Square House, Bloomsbury: all 'Queen Anne' buildings vacated.
1948	PGO takes on payment of NHS pensions.
1949	Occupation of Russell Square House complete.
	Machine class introduced in PGO.
1951	Creation of first promotion board.
1954	Mitre House occupied.
	War memorial unveiled.
1956	Five day working week begins.
	Monthly payment introduced for teachers' pensions.
	1-6 Tavistock Square occupied.

	Withdrawal of cash payment for new pensioners.
1957	Mitre House vacated.
	Mechanisation of pensions begins.
	Withdrawal of cash payment to other departments.
1958	Installation of EMPs.
1959	Salaries first paid to bank accounts.
1962	Computer study group set up.
1963	Installation of ICT 558 computers.
	Dispersal exercise begins.
1964	Payment of pensions to bank accounts introduced.
	Publication of first Penguide.
	Old Post Office occupied.
1965	Goffs Park House occupied.
1966	1-6 Tavistock Square vacated.
	Sussex House occupied.
	Building of Sutherland House begins.
1967	Drill Hall occupied.
	First occupants move to Sutherland House.
	Check digits allocated to pension references.
1968	Installation of ICL System 4 computer.
	Main part of Sutherland House occupied.
	First sports afternoon at Crawley.
1969	Banking and pension systems begin on PANDA.
	Burroughs MICR readers installed.
	Staff inspections begin.
1970	Scottish teachers' pensions transferred to Scottish Education Department.
1971	Decimalisation.
	Job Appraisal Reviews introduced.
	Eagle House occupied: Russell Square House vacated.
	Publication of Compendium.
1972	Internal Audit team set up.
	Customs and Excise, Inland Revenue and QLTR pensions, and Private Car allowances taken on.
	Crown and County Courts banking work taken on.
	PGO payroll taken over by Chessington Computer Centre.
1974	Desk calculators introduced on pension sections.
	Processor controlled keystations installed in data preparation section.
	Quality control introduced.
1975	Weekly pensions computerised.
	Ledger sheets discontinued.
1976	Automatic substitution for EOs begins experimentally.
	Data processor grades introduced.
	Plantime equipment installed.
	ICL 2900 computer delivered.
	Sutherland House extension occupied.
	Paid payable order records microfilmed.
1977	IBM MICR readers installed.
	APEX system goes live.

	Take-on of navy and air force other ranks pensions from MOD.
1978	PGO Administration vote set up. Forestry Commission pensions taken on.
1979	First pension payments by BACS. Teachers' 'island' pensions transferred to island authorities. GMP introduced. New banking and pensions systems implemented. Strike of computer operators halts banking work.
1980	Bank of England takes on receipt of lodgment: Eagle House vacated. Publication of new Penguide.
1981	Strike of computer operators halts pension issues and banking work: manual emergency system set up. Cash payment of wages discontinued.
1982	Night security service privatised. PGO connected to GTN.
1983	Requirement for periodic declarations relaxed. Computerised index of pensions implemented. Privatisation of pension services considered by independent consultants. Bank of England begins to produce lodgment tapes.
1984	Issue and payment of teachers' lump sums transferred to Department of Education and Science, and teachers' awards first received on magnetic tape. Word processor installed.
1985	Financial Management system implemented. All pensions postcoded: new despatch equipment installed. Agreement on New Technology ratified by Departmental Whitley Council. Publication of booklet to commemorate 150th anniversary of the PGO's creation.

INDEX